THE MORALITY OF THE COLOR LINE

An Examination of the Right and the Wrong of the Discriminations Against the Negro in the United States

BY

REV. FRANCIS J. GILLIGAN, S. T. L.

OF THE
ARCHDIOCESE OF SAINT PAUL.

A Dissertation Submitted to the Faculty of Sacred Sciences of the Catholic University of America in partial fulfillment of the requirements for the degree of Doctor of Sacred Theology

NEGRO UNIVERSITIES PRESS
NEW YORK

Originally published in 1928
by Catholic University of America, Washington, D.C.

Reprinted 1969 by
Negro Universities Press
A DIVISION OF GREENWOOD PUBLISHING CORP.
NEW YORK

SBN 8371-2353-4

PRINTED IN UNITED STATES OF AMERICA

To

ARCHBISHOP DOWLING

in

Reverence and Gratitude

CONTENTS

CONTENTS

PREFACE

The Negroes constitute approximately one-tenth of the population of the United States. Against them flourish strong prejudices and numerous discriminations which isolate them from the other inhabitants and which partially thwart their progress. Those discriminations have been inaugurated, and are now perpetuated by white persons who, to a large extent, profess Christianity. Obviously, such conditions have occasioned a moral problem which is deserving of serious and immediate attention.

Some white Christians are serenely unconscious of any incongruity between their profession of Christianity and their treatment of the Negroes. Contacts with the Negroes have been regarded as a field completely divorced from the sphere in which moral precepts must be observed. A greater number of white Christians, however, have been embarrassed and disquieted by a consciousness of the incongruity. But, although disquieted, they feel that some discriminations are morally justifiable because of the striking racial differences. Yet they are very uncertain as to what actions are right and what actions are wrong. There are few authoritative treatises in which they may seek explicit guidance. The treatment of the problem from a Christian view-point has been limited largely to an inspirational appeal.

The absence of detailed and specific moral instruction on the American race problem is not an exceptional condition. It is a reflection of an attitude which numerous Christians have adapted toward social contacts. Probably it is a back-wash from the Indifferentism of the last century which prompted some to formulate the ethical principles of Christianity in terms of a comfortable ambiguity. Such an attitude is not Catholic. It differs considerably from that which prevailed in great Christian centuries, such as the Middle Ages, when the writers endeavored to translate Christian principles into a code of practical ethics sufficiently precise to be applied to the dusty world of warehouse and farm.

In the volume in hand, the author has attempted to apply to the American race problem the method used by the Christian writers of other centuries in their treatment of social problems. An effort has been made to examine the discriminations against the Negroes in terms of strict obligation; to determine not only the heroic works which a Christian should perform in order to be perfect, but the actions which must be fulfilled if the Christian would attain eternal life. The hope is entertained that the volume will have value in that it may provoke discussion and induce more competent students to examine the field.

While an examination of the moral implications constitutes the main object of the book, the history of various phases of the problem has been given that the reader might acquire a sympathetic approach to the problem. Data on the intelligence of the Negroes, on their environment, and on other social forces relative to their life have been presented because moral judgments are frequently conditioned by such factors.

The author wishes to record here his indebtedness to Rev. Dr. John A. Ryan, who suggested the work, and whose advice and assistance have been frequent and invaluable. Also he desires to avail himself of this occasion to express gratitude to the members of the faculty of Sacred Sciences of the Catholic University for their many kindnesses; to Bishop Feehan of Fall River who graciously granted several important permissions; and to Archbishop Dowling of Saint Paul who manifested an encouraging interest in the work and who made it possible for the author to engage in three years of graduate study at the University.

CHAPTER I

HISTORIC ORIGINS

THE NEGRO IN AFRICA

The Negroes and the Europeans were brought into contact during the early part of the fifteenth century. In striking contrast to the high civilization achieved by the white race in Europe, the Negroes were living on a barbaric level. Yet in appraising the condition of the African Negro of that period, many white Americans are prone to neglect two important facts.

The first is that the failure of the African Negroes to build a civilization can be explained in some measure by their physical environment. A larger section of Africa than of any other continent lies within the torrid zone. Much of the territory is impenetrable because of the swamps and heavy tropical growth. These two factors, in addition to the abundance of food, could easily discourage the initiative and the creative efforts which have occasioned the origin of native civilizations. But cultures and civilizations usually are not built solely upon the creative work of one group. More commonly they are a mosaic formed from practices and customs which a race has acquired from contact with other races. In that respect also the Negroes were handicapped, since their physical surroundings did not permit them to borrow extensively from other races. To a large extent they were isolated. Other peoples were barred from Africa bcause the unbroken coast line offered few sheltering harbors and because the rivers, with the exception of the Nile, were not navigable. Those natural boundaries were supplemented by two great deserts and mountain ranges. So for thousands of years the people of Africa, with the exception of those north of the desert, lacked contact with other races and dropped behind the progress of the world.[1] One evidence of the magnitude of the handicap presented by the physical environment is that the colonization and exploitation of Africa by Europeans has been slow, even though Africa's coast lines were explored earlier than those of America and even though Africa is richer in resources.

A second fact neglected by many Americans is that the Negroes, though uncivilized, developed a notable culture before the fifteenth century. An American scientist has declared that, "any impartial student must admit that the Negro in Africa was culturally superior to the Indian of the United States."[2] Concerning the Negro's ability for political organization, Weatherford writes: "Wherever the conditions of communication permitted, the Negroes built large empires which, while more primitive than European states, nevertheless compared favorably with many of the white man's governments. Unfortunately for the reputation of the Negro the fullest information which we have had pertains to the coast tribes where all the conditions militated against the building of large empires."[3] There is also an abundance of evidence which indicates that the Negroes had acquired considerable skill in the manufacture of iron, cutlery, pottery, and in the art of embroidery. The products of the primitive Negro wood-carver, weaver, and potter were original in form, were skillful in execution, and gave evidence of a love of labor. The nature of their economic life depended upon the locality. In the west there was very little farming or grazing because food could be had for the plucking and because raiment was unnecessary. But in other sections many tribes engaged in cattle raising and in farming. It is especially

1 Cf. Keane, "Man, Past and Present," p. 40.
2 *Publications of the American Sociological Society*, vol. 19, p. 68.
3 "The Negro from Africa to America," p. 34.

worthy of note that a closely knit system of markets flourished among them. Brisk trading in iron hoes, garden products, and baskets was carried on at regular intervals. Their thrift and keenness amazed many travelers.[4]

Their moral life differed sharply, of course, from that of the white Christians of the period. Slavery, superstition, fetishism, idleness, and cruelty flourished among them. Yet they were not as completely unmoral and as degenerate as they have been pictured. Lying and thieving within their own groups were unknown before the time the Europeans oppressed them. One early traveler wrote of them: "In all our trading with them we never sustained the loss of one bead. They retain the first incorrupt innocence of man, a people approaching in some degree near Adam."[5] Moreover sexual promiscuity was not as common as one might expect. The family, though frequently polygamous, was the pillar upon which all social life depended. Marriage was surrounded by many prohibitions and, though unstable, existed by virtue of a real contract. Polyandry was practically unknown. The sexes were separated until the age of puberty and then they were initiated in the mysteries of the tribe and expected to marry. If a child was born to a girl prior to her initiation, it was destroyed. Adultery was punished. A strict taboo was enforced to prevent consanguineous alliances, and to prevent conjugal relations during pregnancy and nursing.[6] Indeed, too great emphasis cannot be placed upon the fact that their essential social institutions were safeguarded from the passions of individuals and their sexual tendencies restrained by an elaborate system of taboos and interdicts woven about their primitive life. Those moral restraints which are thought indispensible for the social life of today were guaranteed by their primitive group customs.

---

4 Cf. *The American Anthropologist,* Jan. 1924, pp. 59-62.
5 Muntz, "Race Contact," p. 226.
6 Le Roy, "The Religion of the Primitives," pp. 71, sq.

The Negro from Africa to America

In the year 1445 on the west coast of Africa, the modern Europeans, the white race, came into contact for the first time with the Negroes. Immediately the white race adopted a policy typical of that attitude which they were to follow for the succeeding four centuries;—they enslaved the Negroes and removed them from the continent. The white race was strong and wise with the knowledge and the experience of many races which had lived before them. The Negroes were weak and ignorant from isolation. Great opportunities were opened to the white race. They could have undertaken the tedious but noble task of imparting to that undeveloped branch of the human race the knowledge which they had acquired from other peoples. They could have undertaken the delicate and complex work of gradually substituting Christian moral convictions for the taboos which restrained the passions of the blacks. But the opportunities were neglected, though the Spanish and Portuguese governments did strive to stifle their consciences by baptizing the Africans. The European races, the Spanish, the Dutch, the English, sought to capitalize the weaknesses and the ignorance of the blacks. Goaded on by a lust for riches they thought only of using the blacks as means for increasing their wealth. At the time of the first contact a policy was inaugurated which developed into the nefarious slave-trade, the slave-trade which injured the Negro race almost irreparably. Some realization of that injury may be gained by noting the magnitude of the traffic.

Prince Henry of Portugal inaugurated in 1445 the first systematic movement for exporting Negroes from Africa to Europe. His efforts were so fruitful that by the year of 1460 he was selling as many as eight hundred slaves annually in Portugal and in Spain. A large proportion of those Negroes were set to work on the large estates vacated by the Moors. With the founding of the Spanish colonies in the New World an acute need for cheap labor arose. The native Indians were enslaved but their fierce spirit rendered them unfit for such a mode of life. The colonists looked enviously toward the African Negroes whom they had seen in Spain and Portugal. The Spanish Crown after some hesitancy yielded to the pressure and in 1501 permitted the Negroes born in Christian lands to be carried to Hispaniola. But that restriction was soon cancelled, and the Negroes were transported directly from Africa to America. The traffic grew so rapidly that in 1518 it was recorded that over five thousand black slaves were sold to the colonists.[7]

After the defeat of the Spanish Armada the Dutch seized the Portugese stations on the west coast, and the Danes, the French and the English sought to gain control of the trade which was the badge of maritime supremacy. Any vestige of humaneness that had lingered in the trade was crushed by that competition. The English finally gained the supremacy, and under their direction the trade assumed unprecedented proportions. The Royal African Company of England sold in the year 1672 two thousand slaves to Jamaica alone. In 1771 the number of slave ships registered from the port of Liverpool was reported as one hundred and seven with a capacity for 29,250 slaves. There were also slave ships registered in other cities; for example in the same year fifty-eight sailed from London and twenty-eight from Bristol. Besides the English ships there were many vessels from New England engaged in the trade, for the Yankees had been attracted by the lucrative profits. Historians record that Newport became a replica of Liverpool.[8] The slave-trade made millionaires in America, in England and on the continent. It brought prosperity to the white shipbuilder, the whiskey distiller, and the white manufacturer. But it despoiled and partially destroyed the Negro race.

The Negroes who were sold to American colonists during the eighteenth century differed greatly from the

---

7 Phillips, "American Negro Slavery," chapters I and II, passim.
8 Phillips, op. cit., pp. 20-45.

Negroes who had resided in Africa prior to the ravaging of the west coast by the whites. The slave-trade had despoiled the African Negroes of their primitive culture and had demoralized them. The slave-trade had kept Western Africa in a constant state of war. The coast tribes, dazzled by the white trader's wares and assisted by his weapons, continuously provoked war with the interior tribes, and secured slaves by scouring the interior.[9] Peaceful villages were surprised and fired by night. The aged were slaughtered and the youths enslaved. Many of the slaves sold on the coast had been captured by slave hunters far within the interior and marched through hundreds of miles of jungle.

The disintegration suffered by Negroid peoples as a consequence of the slave-trade was similar in nature to that sustained by highly civilized peoples that have been subjected to prolonged wars and invasions. Their skill in peaceful pursuits, such as weaving and basketry declined. Their social institutions crumbled and their traditions were forgotten. But a more serious disruption followed in their moral life. The restraints upon the passions of the Negroes had been dependent upon primitive social institutions. These customs were braces which propped their character. The experience of the individual natives had been too limited to incite them to rationalize or generalize about these customs. The slaves sold in America had been suddenly wrenched from their villages, and marched in coffles to the coast. There they had been separated from their own tribesmen, graded for sale, and herded into slave ships. Frequently the blacks crowded in the ships were as much strangers to one another as they were to their white captors, because they were members of different tribes and possessed different dialects.[10] When the slaves were disembarked upon American soil, the external braces which had sustained their actions and moral life were missing. In a

---

9 Muntz, "Race Contact," p. 210.
10 Phillips, "American Negro Slavery," pp. 34, 455.

strange land, coercively subjected to laws and customs far different from those of their ancestral country, they were deprived of an incentive to conformity, and inevitably they surrendered to their impulses and passions. Boas states, "the tearing away from African soil and the consequent loss of old standards of life, which were replaced by the dependence of slavery, are sufficient to explain the inferiority of the status of the Negro race." [11]

The Negro Slave in the United States

The Negroes are frequently regarded as the beneficiaries of American slavery. The institution is thought of as a rigorous but wholesome discipline which prepared the undeveloped Africans for participation in the life of a highly-civilized nation. Undoubtedly after the great wrong of transporting these people to this country had been committed, some special system of training should have been devised. It must be admitted, also, that the Negroes were benefited in many ways by dwelling in the midst of the American people. Every man is to a large extent the product of his environment. They were rescued from superstition, fetishism, and a fondness for magic. They acquired some of the fundamentals of civilization and a knowledge of the English language. Their health in the new continent was safeguarded by the sanitary regulations of the plantations. Some acquaintance with the consoling truths of Christianity and with Christian moral institutions, such as monogamous family life, was acquired. Yet not one of these benefits was inseparable from slavery. All could have been secured under another system of training. Actually American slavery, while bestowing some advantages upon the Negroes, tended to train them in evil habits and to unfit them for active participation in American life at the time of their emancipation. For the development of a strong Christian character, American slavery did not offer the proper training. Murphy voiced the conviction of many of his

---

11 Boas, "The Mind of the Primitive Man," p. 272.

Southern associates when he declared "as a school for freedom slavery was necessarily inadequate."[12]

The Negroes were ignorant when they were brought here. American slavery tended to crystallize that ignorance. With the exception of the twenty-five years which preceded the Revolutionary War, the constant practice of the slave-holding class was to prevent the Negroes from acquiring knowledge. Stringent regulations were enacted in the Southern States forbidding any person to teach a Negro to read or to write. The slave owners realized that the existence of the institution of slavery depended upon the ignorance of the Negro. The statutes of the State of Georgia were typical of the laws of the other States. In Georgia the first law forbidding the imparting of knowledge to the Negroes was enacted at the end of the eighteenth century. In 1824 it was revised and a penalty of $500 was added for its violation. In 1833 it was again amended so that even the master who permitted a slave to transact business for him in writing committed a misdemeanor.[13] The success of that effort to keep the Negroes in ignorance may be gauged by the fact that as late as 1880 seventy per cent of the colored people were illiterate.[14] Elwang, writing of conditions a decade later, stated, "persons of African descent, either slave or free, who could read were always striking exceptions to the prevailing illiteracy and mental stupor."[15]

The great evil involved in the policy of *crystallizing* the Negro's ignorance may be more keenly appreciated if we remember that it accentuated differences between the white man and the Negro. During another age, the effects might not have been so disastrous. But it occurred during a time when education was esteemed by the multitude, when the white man was acquiring greater plasticity. To the Negro was denied the rich social heri-

---

12 "The Basis of Ascendancy," p. 27.
13 Stroud, "Sketches of Laws Relating to Slavery," p. 64.
14 Hart, "Slavery and Abolition," p. 94.
15 Elwang, "The Negroes of Columbia Missouri," p. 38.

tage of the people among whom he lived. His mind was left unexercised. Education, the great force which is so powerful in equalizing racial differences, was denied him.

There was little in American slavery which tended to substitute a Christian family life for the polygamous institution destroyed by the slave-trade. Seldom was any distinction made between male and female. "On all plantations women worked alongside the men even to the extent of drawing the plow." The women, with the exception of those actually nursing children, left the cabins before daybreak with the men and remained with them until sundown. Breakfast and dinner were served in the fields. The infants and the children, too young to be employed profitably, were kept in a nursery and cared for by a disabled slave.[16] Moreover, there was little law or ceremony to impress the slaves with the seriousness of the marriage contract. In most States slave marriages did not enjoy legal recognition.

Furthermore, the possibility of being separated from their families by sale discouraged the slaves from regarding their marital contracts as indissoluble. It is maintained that the frequency of the sales of slaves has been grossly exaggerated. It is probable that there was some exaggeration. Nevertheless the possibility of being sold was always present to the Negro. By law he was subject to sale at all times and in every community there were constantly some exchanges of such property. Moreover the sale of slaves was not as infrequent as some writers profess. Channing declares: "thousands were sold Southward yearly from the upper States. It could not have been otherwise."[17] From Washington alone during the thirties and forties, approximately a thousand slaves were shipped yearly. The sales within the various Southern States were also numerous if one may judge from the advertisements in the Southern papers. The sale of town slaves must have been large

---

16 Hart, op. cit., p. 99. Cf. Olmstead, "A Journey in the Seaboard Slave States," vol. II, p. 11.
17 Channing, "History of the United States," vol. VI, p. 22.

because a lawyer or a doctor had little choice but to sell the extra slaves that were unnecessary in his domestic establishment. Hart has summarized his treatment of the slave's social life by the observation: "Slavery made a real family life almost impossible except on the smaller plantations where one or more families of slaves was the only valuable asset of the owners."[18]

American slavery placed few restraints upon the Negro's sex life and failed to offer any efficacious substitute for the taboos and interdicts of the African village. Little information is available about the relations of blacks among themselves during the slave days. It is probable that few restrictions were placed upon them, since much of the white man's concern was exhausted in securing from the Negro a day's labor. However, it is quite certain that there was considerable illicit intercourse between the races. Phillips, who is usually cautious, states that concubinage was fairly frequent.[19] Olmstead made a similar judgment. Rhodes in his History of the United States quotes Madison's sister as saying, "we Southern ladies are complimented with the names of wives, but we are only the mistresses of seraglios." The same author cites as the reason for the readiness with which the colored maiden surrendered to the advances of the white man the attitude of instinctive submission which the white man had inculcated in the black. Under the law no slave might raise his hand against a white person unless his life was in danger.[20] Woofter has observed in this connection: "The African system was one of polygamous clans. The slave was uprooted from an existence under this plan and placed upon a plantation where monogamy was theoretically demanded but seldom expected. This amounted to a new polygamy with all the evils and none of the benefits of the African system. The African system was a complete

18 Hart, op. cit., p. 102.
19 Phillips, op. cit., p. 194.
20 Rhodes, "History of the United States from the Missouri Compromise," vol. I, p. 500.

protection for girls, and a strong protection for wives against everything but the tyranny of the husband. But the plantation polygamy left the chastity of the Negro women absolutely unprotected in law and little guarded in custom."[21]

Practically no training in industriousness and foresight was given to the Negro during the slave period. Long before the Civil War a correspondent for the New York Times wrote: "the slave is without motive, without plan, without inducement to exertion. His food, his clothing, and all his wants are supplied without care on his part and when they are supplied he has nothing more to hope for. He can make no provision for old age, he can lay up nothing for his children. What cares he whether his labor is productive or unproductive? His principle care seems to be to accomplish just as little as possible."[22] The Negroes could not aspire to become overseers because the law forbade it. Many of them were forbidden to cultivate garden patches, because it tempted them to reserve their strength for the night. They were forbidden to hire out their free time for the same reason. The task system, also, which was designed to remedy this deficiency of slavery was ineffective.[23]

Even the possibility of gaining his liberty by self purchase was so remote for the Negro that it was incapable of stimulating his labor. Most slaves who became free were liberated by the hands of their master. But the process of manumission was always restricted. In more than half of the States the emancipated were obliged to leave the State. In 1850 only one out of every 2,181 slaves was manumitted, and in 1860 one out of every 1,309. Moreover, if a Negro were emancipated the danger of being kidnapped was imminent. Since complexion gave presumption of slave status and custody gave color

---

21 Woofter, "The Basis of Racial Adjustment," p. 227.
22 Cf. Olmstead, vol. II, p. 12.
23 Phillips, op. cit., p. 412.

of ownership, the possibility of redress through law was faint.[24]

Along with the absence of training in foresight their initiative was crushed. The Negro's actions were curtailed and restricted at every turn. By law slaves were forbidden to meet in large numbers, they were forbidden to keep a gun, to be on horseback without permission, to fish with a seine, to be away from the plantation. To these prohibitions may be added a series of arbitrary restraints imposed by individuals, since all whites were permitted and in some instances required to exercise police power over the slaves. Under such conditions only two alternatives were open, either to risk death by running away or to degenerate into an automaton.

Their religious training was warped during the slave period because the white ministers engaged by the planters were prone to overstress the virtue of obedience. "What faults you are guilty of toward your masters are faults against God Himself," was a favorite theme. A disregard for the property of white persons was encouraged since the blacks were not assumed to possess the right of ownership. An incentive to treat their wives and children cruelly was given, since the white race administered brutal and indecent whippings to colored women and men. Other influences could be mentioned. But these are sufficient to suggest the numerous evils involved in American slavery, evils which handicapped and thwarted the development of the colored race within the United States.

The Negro Freedman

Slavery as a legal institution was abolished in the United States at the end of the year 1865. The task of emancipating the slaves presented a grave problem. The successful transformation of a dependent group to the status of a free, industrious, sober people required of the advanced group unity of purpose, patience, enlight-

---

24 Phillips, op. cit, p. 443.

ened direction. But unfortunately the conditions under which the Negroes were liberated were the antithesis of the ideal. The country had been drained by a fratricidal war. The industries in which the blacks had been employed were disorganized. The whites, amidst whom the blacks were to continue to dwell, thought the Negroes were destined to be always the hewers of wood for the white race. The ten years which followed the Civil War were years of social unrest and turmoil, years in which the sectional strife was continued.

The Negroes were freed but, with the exception of the limited work of the Freedmen's Bureau and the activities of Northern missionaries, no systematic provision was made for their direction or education. Inevitably some of them grew restless and refused to work. To protect the public from an alleged menace the Southern States enacted the black code laws which practically reduced the Negro group to serfdom. Those measures were the first of a series which were passed alternately by the Southern States and by the Federal Government, and in which the Negroes were used as tools for promoting the purposes of both groups. Neither the North nor the South were earnestly interested in the Negroes' welfare, but both found in the Negro group a convenient standard about which their sectional strife could be waged. The black code so antagonized leaders of Congress that they sought to punish the South by enacting the Fourteenth and Fifteenth Amendments. They insisted upon giving to the Negroes all the rights and privileges of citizens. They insisted upon perpetuating policies which gave the Negroes political control over the territory in which they had formerly been slaves. Inevitably, because of the lack of training the Negroes abused that power. Inevitably many acquired a false concept of freedom and education. At the end of the decade the North finally tired of interference and abandoned the Negroes to their former masters. By the use of force the freedmen were quickly driven from power, suppressed, and then ignored.

Disfranchised and oppressed, the Negroes then tended to draw away from the whites in all but economic contacts. Assisted by a few philanthropists and missionaries, they struggled to transform themselves from a servile, dependent class to a self-sustaining, independent people. Under the leadership of men of their own race, such as Booker T. Washington, they strove to acquire the virtues of freedmen. They endeavored to develop a sense of racial pride. At a great sacrifice they struggled to give to their children, from their limited financial resources, the education which the whites had denied.

The progress achieved by the Negroes during that period was phenomenal. When the Civil War ended they were as a class illiterate and poor. Sixty years later 700,000 Negroes owned their homes, and the colored as a group had accumulated wealth of two billion dollars.[25] Ninety per cent are now able to read and write. Thirty-nine Negroes have been awarded the degree of Doctor of Philosophy by leading American Universities. There are several Negro professors in universities such as Harvard and Chicago. In the field of letters, poetry, and science they have made valuable contributions. The writings of such Negroes as Du Bois and Alain Locke, a Rhodes scholar, have won from impartial critics unstinted praise for the brilliancy and purity of their English. The novels of Walter H. White and James Weldon Johnson have gained for those Negroes enviable reputations. Countee Cullen and Langston Hughes have published books of verse which have been rated as best sellers in the world of poetry. During the year 1927 two of the most artistic plays on Broadway were presented by colored casts. Their exceptional musical successes are typified in the achievement of Roland Hayes.

In the economic and social fields great conquests have, also, been made. For example, in the Cleveland Hardware Company both the chief chemist and the metallurgist are Negroes. In New York City a Negro has the

---

25 "Negro Year Book," p. 2.

contract for building all the concrete moulds for a new seven million dollar hospital. In the same city over 600 Negroes are engaged as public school teachers.[26] There is, moreover, a rapidly increasing number of families of the Negro bourgeoisie that live in expensively appointed homes, have maids and chauffeurs, send their sons to Columbia and their daughters to Barnard or Vassar. They invest in antiques and rare objects of art, summer in Maine, and travel occasionally in Europe. There are individual Negroes who have reaped fortunes from wise investments,—fortunes which have been built around the nest eggs salted away by the preceding generation of washer women and Pullman porters.[27]

Despite this phenomenal progress the Negroes find that they are still severely handicapped and restricted by prejudice and race hatred. In factories, in educational institutions, in public places they are confronted with that great composite of discriminations which is designated as the race problem.

The early colonists created a grave problem for themselves and for their descendants by importing into the country a large number of Negroes who were at the opposite pole of development and who differed from the other inhabitants in skin color, in physical features, and in customs. Since striking differences usually beget prejudices and aversions, it was almost inevitable that such dissimilarities among the subjects of a nation should furnish perennial occasions for internal friction and distrust. Their descendants, after the War of Independence, multiplied the problem a hundred-fold by sanctioning Negro slavery in the Federal Constitution. By thus crystallizing the ignorance and the weaknesses of the Negroes and thwarting their development, they accentuated the racial differences and increased the prejudice. The Fathers of the Republic made the black skin the badge of the slave and of the servant. They

---

[26] *Opportunity,* Jan., 1928, p. 12.
[27] *The World Tomorrow,* Nov., 1927, p. 465.

trained their own race to regard the Negroes as a permanent servile class. In turn, their children further aggravated the problem by provoking a situation which involved the hurried emancipation of the Negroes as a war measure and then the employment of them as a weapon for punishing the recalcitrant South. The white Southerners were induced to regard the Negroes as potential enemies of their welfare.

CHAPTER II

PROPOSED SOLUTIONS AND THEIR ALLEGED JUSTIFICATION

For the great race problem which has vexed and haunted the American people a variety of immediate solutions have been suggested. Probably expatriation has been the favored solution. As early as 1773 an effort was made to collect funds for the purpose of establishing a colony on the west coast of Africa for freed Negroes. From that time until the Civil War the advisability and the advantage of such a movement was mooted by many individuals, some as prominent as Jefferson. The movement was not only discussed but actually attempted. One prosperous Negro from the city of New Bedford carried at his own expense more than nine families to Africa. The American Colonization Society with the assistance of the Federal Government established a colony and transported approximately 15,000 free Negroes to the West Coast. Lincoln during the Civil War advocated a settlement in the West Indies, and Congress voted $600,000 for the furtherance of the project. But both the project of the American Colonization Society and that of Lincoln were unsuccessful, and after the War they passed rapidly into the realm of theory.[1]

Throughout the last twenty years white writers, especially English travelers such as Archer in his "Through Afro-America," have advocated that all Negroes within breeding ages should be compelled to migrate to some African settlement which the American government would develop. Cox, a Virginian, in his work "White America" has stressed the feasibility of the project,

1 Bassett, "A Short History of the United States," p. 428.

and as an analogy cited the success achieved by America in transporting millions of troops to France during the World War. Other theorists, such as Gregory in his "Menace of Color," have advocated the segregation of the Negro population within one or two Southern states. The suggestion has even been made that the Fourteenth and Fifteenth Amendments should be repealed, and that th Negro should be made a ward of the government, such as the Indian. Then, instead of being content with a nominal equality, an effort could be made to raise the actual standard of the race.

The perpetration of all of these schemes is physically possible. But the attempted enactment of any one is so far removed from the realm of probability that the discussion of the grave moral problems involved in such policies seems unnecessary. "There are some people," writes Dr. Tannenbaum, "who are still talking about the removal of the Negro to Africa. That is one of the things that will never be done. The reason is that it cannot be done. There will never be possible in America a policy so consistent and deliberate as that involved in the transportation of ten million human beings to a barren country. It would, of course, take an enormous effort nationally and ten million human beings are not merely shipped out like ten million grains. . . . The Negro is so well rooted here both politically and economically that the wrenching of internal social life in America resulting from any such deliberate policy would be appalling. It would be equivalent to a revolution or a war and still leave the problem unsolved. . . . Another solution of a similar type is that suggested by people who would give the Negro a State, move him there, and let him govern himself, a State in the union hermetically sealed up for generations. If people were not such eternal romanticists one would simply have to laugh at the suggestion. It involves all the difficulties of the African project and a great many more—one of them the simple fact that there is an increasing tide in American life and that there are no internal barriers that would sustain the eternal pushing of human flux to a common level."[2]

Of much greater practical importance than the proposed solutions are the reasons or factors alleged in justification for such movements. For these same reasons are frequently cited as warrants for policies which, though less drastic, affect the Negro deeply. It is affirmed, that the Negroes are inherently inferior in mental powers to the whites, that they are incorrigibly immoral, that the races cannot live together peacefully and happily. Many white Americans accept these contentions as truths and regulate their attitude toward individual Negroes and toward face relations accordingly. Therefore, some examination of those contentions should be undertaken.

The Mental Inferiority of the Negro

The Negroes in the United States, it is held, are not only inferior in regard to education and mental development but are also inferior to the whites in native mental ability. During the slave period in America the assumption of the Negro's inferiority was generally accepted, and that assumption was advanced as a justification for slavery.[3] After the war the assumption persisted. In the scientific books of the last quarter of the ninteenth century the Negro's inferiority was often defended as a thesis. The advocates of white supremacy were able to quote Wymen of Harvard and numerous other scholars to substantiate their position. Today scientists would discard, almost completely, both the forms of argument and the data used by those scholars. Nevertheless, the radical inferiority of the Negro is still widely defended in scientific circles.

One argument, which appealed strongly to writers both popular and scientific, is founded upon the Negro's cultural sterility. "The fact," wrote Murphy, a Southern philosopher famed for his tolerance, "at the background

---

2 Tannenbaum, "Darker Phases of the South," p. 154.
3 Hart, "Slavery and Abolition," p. 142.

of every Negro, however, wise, or well educated, or brave, or good, is contemporary Africa. At no point in the history of states or in the development of human families does a demonstration of his social capacity or of his collective achievement in art or letters or government look out from the familiar possibilities of his genius."[4]

The cultural sterility of the Negro relative to that of other races must be recognized, with some qualifications, as a fact. The contention of Murphy and others is both attractive and plausible. Yet despite its plausibility many eminent scientists deny, and properly so, the validity of deducing the Negro's inferiority from his cultural sterility. Their opinion has been thus summarized by Dr. Reuter: "A single contest may determine the superiority of one athlete over another. But we would not pronounce one superior to the other because of their relative positions at any moment before the end of the race, or without taking into account their starting points, the difficulty of their routes, the accidents of their journey, the incentive to exertion. . . . No fact is more firmly established than that the cultural positions of races change. The fact that a race has a low culture during one historic era is not evidence that the status will remain. . . . Civilizations of a high order existed in Egypt for some thousands of years, during which time the culture of the Greeks and Romans idled at the barbaric level. It is not probable that any Egyptian believed the race that was later to produce the Athenian civilization of the age of Pericles had a mental calibre and cultural capacity equal to his own. The Egyptians disposed of the capacity of the Greeks and Romans to produce a civilization on the ground that they had never done so, just as these Greeks and Romans in the days of their glory disposed of our barbarian ancestors, and just as we, in the intolerance of our historic moment are disposed to dismiss the Negroes and the Indians."[5]

---

4 "The Basis, of Ascendancy," p. 42.
5 "The American Race Problem," p. 74.

In the light of the increasing popularity of the evolutionary hypothesis, various popular writers have resuscitated an old argument, and have inferred the inferiority of the Negro from those peculiar morphological traits which white people regard as brutal. Those traits, it has been argued, indicate that the Negro occupies a lower place in the zoological series and has a greater resemblance of the anthropoid. But the argument, to the extent that is founded on general traits, is not well grounded. While in prognathism, cranial massiveness, arm length, and receding forehead the Negro appears to be more closely related to the higher anthropoids, in other respects the white man appears to occupy a lower place on the development scale. For example, the full red everted lips of the Negro are perhaps the most human of all physical characteristics in the sense that they stand most markedly contrasted to the bloodless lips of the anthropoids.

Since the War the proof of the Negro's inferiority has been drawn more commonly from the studies made with psychological tests. These tests were organized for the first time in their essential form by the French physician, Binet, about the year 1905. In subsequent years they were adapted to this country by Goddard in New York and by Terman in California. They have been used very widely in school work and have been in a process of constant revision and refinement. The aim of the test is to measure not knowledge but native intelligence, or the ability "of an organism to adjust itself adequately to new situations." Between 1916 and 1925 approximately twenty-five scholarly studies of the Negro were made with these tests. Various forms were used and the results differed widely among themselves. Yet all the tests, as they were summarized by Dr. Garth in "The Psychological Bulletin," agree in that they indicate the Negro group to be inferior to the white group.[6] A considerable number of American psychologists and educators hold that these devices actually measure in

6 *Psychological Bulletin*, June, 1925, vol. 22, p. 343.

some degree native intelligence. They receive the studies as scientific proof of the Negro's inferiority. However, the scholars who have labored persistently in the perfection of these mental measurements do not place the extreme interpretation upon the results which have characterized the statements of many popular writers and pseudo-scientists. Pintner, in a review of the problems encountered in the organization of such tests has written: "Different sections of a city differ greatly in intelligence and so do different rural communities. The existence of such differences need not make us give up as hopeless the standardization of intelligence tests but the knowledge that they exist should keep us from being dogmatic and from regarding any scale as being a complete and final rod of intelligence."[7] Chapman has observed: "contrasting the colored population of the United States with the whole population after allowing for differences in opportunity, motivation, and the tradition of the two groups, we may legitimately assume that the white population is in the intelligence scale a year or a year and a half superior to the pure stock of the colored race. But the overlapping in the intellectual status of the two races is so great as to nullify the popular conception of the extreme difference of the two groups."[8]

Dr. Estabrooks of Colgate University writes that opposing the members of the psychological school which sponsors intelligence tests: "we have probably the majority of the psychological school and practically all the anthropologists who view their results and conclusions with open suspicion. The reason for this open suspicion is obvious. The critics have very grave doubts whether we are able to measure the intelligence of any group of people with tests devised to gauge that of another group. The environment of the two may be entirely different, their social customs and traditions may vary widely, they may not even speak the same language or may

---

7 Pintner, "Intelligence Testing," p. 86.
8 Chapman, "Principles of Education," p. 179.

speak it with different degrees of facility."[9] A distinguished anthropologist, Dr. Lowie, holds that the protagonists of the tests assume what is to be proved. "Admitting as they must that an empirical test cannot eliminate the environmental factor they decree that certain observed differences are too great to be explained by environmental differences, hence are evidences of hereditary differences. The illegitimacy of such reasoning is apparent as soon as it is couched in clear language. . . . The environmental factor must be taken into account and unless we devise methods for its quantitative determination let us hold our tongues concerning differences."[10]

The writers who challenge the intelligence tests as valid proofs of the native inferiority of the Negro do not insist that all races are intrinsically equal. They admit the possibilities of race differences. They acknowledge that the white group in America is actually superior to the colored group in the matter of education and mental development. They merely claim that the native inferiority of the Negro group has not been proved scientifically. They are scientific agnostics in regard to the doctrine of white supremacy. It is with their opinion that we are inclined to concur.

There are many white persons, who, on the authority of the other school of psychologists, hold the opposite opinion. Obviously, they are free to do so. Yet, in the minds of such persons the four following truths should be capitalized. In the first place, absolutely no data have been advanced to prove that the Negroes are so innately inferior to the whites that they are incapable of acquiring the education and the social attitude which is essential for the fulfillment of the duties of citizenship. As Chapman has observed: "under a universal system of education, the differences of mental age are not greatly noticeable. It means that the Negro race will never in proportion contribute as many great intel-

---

[9] *The American Naturalist,* vol. LXII, pp. 76-87.
[10] *The American Anthropologist,* vol. XXV, p. 298.

lectual leaders. But it does not mean that the race lacks sufficient intelligence to fulfill the prerogatives and the duties of citizenship or that they will be incapable of taking an active role in the economic and industrial life."[11]

Secondly, a possibility exists that the mental power of the Negro group, if it is inferior, may improve. Boas, who has probably proved that physical traits are changed by environment, maintains that mental traits may also change under the same stimulus. "From these facts," he writes, "we must conclude that the fundamental traits of the mind which are closely correlated with the physical condition of the body and whose development continues over many years after physical growth has ceased are the more subject to far-reaching changes."[12] Furthermore, in addition to the mental powers transmitted by inheritance, there is transferred by formal and informal education a social heritage which affects deeply the daily life of man. That the American Negro has not received his proportionate share of that heritage no one seriously denies. What effect that heritage will have on the Negro is difficult to ascertain. Oldham has observed: "It is impossible to determine with any accuracy the part played by each of the two factors, heredity and tradition, so inextricably are they interwoven in human history. It may be noted that all attempts to explain national characteristics by hereditary racial differences have been singularly unsuccessful."[13]

Thirdly, the psychologists do not profess to have proved the Negro to be inferior in all mental traits but only in certain specific ones such as judgment, in ability to define and analyze exactly, in abstract reasoning. The tests, in the language of the psychologists, have been quantitative rather than qualitative. In other respects the Negro group may be superior to the white group, and in those respects they can make a valuable contribution

11 Op. cit., p. 171.
12 Boas, "The Mind of the Primitive Man," p. 62.
13 Oldham, "Christianity and the Race Problem," p. 62.

to American life. Life would assume a most depressing hue if we were forced to live constantly with a race of abstract thinkers. The human mind is endowed with a myriad of traits and no one race has yet shown a proficiency in them all.

Fourthly, the exponents of intelligence tests do not maintain that they have proved each individual Negro inferior to the average white man. Each colored person must be judged on his or her personal merits. Even the most uncompromising exponents of intelligence tests admit that at least one-fourth of the colored group attain or surpass the average median intelligence of the white group. As Dr. Hankins insists: "inferiority and superiority as here used are primarily statistical concepts. They imply as regards hereditary traits a tendency on the part of one group to manifest the measured trait in a form of a distribution characteristically different from the other."[14] "Superiority or inferiority in this sense cannot therefore be imputed to an individual merely because he belongs to the superior or the inferior group. Negroes as a race may be inferior in general intelligence to whites but certain Negroes are distinctly superior to most whites."[15]

The Immorality of the Negro

That the Negro group is incorrigibly immoral is, also, the contention of those who advocate radical solutions such as expatriation. The fact of a greater prevalency of crime among the colored group is unquestionable. In 1910 according to the incomplete statistics relative to the prison population of the United States the ratio per 100,000 for the white population was 114.6 and for the colored 424.6.[16] The prejudice of officials probably accounts for the conviction of some of these Negroes, for they are easily arrested and convicted. Prejudice may also explain in part the abnormal number of Negroes

---

14 Hankins, "The Racial Basis of Civilization," p. 302.
15 Idem, p. 296.
16 Reuter, "The American Race Problem," p. 348.

who are accused of serious crimes. In one year in Detroit of the 130 persons charged with murder seventy-six were Negroes. But only two Negroes were charged with manslaughter while twenty-eight whites were thus accused.[17] But even when due allowance is made for prejudice there undoubtedly flourishes among the colored group a proportionately greater amount of crime. The pertinent question is whether that prevalency of crimes is due to some native weakness of the Negro or to extrinsic factors.

One extrinsic factor for which allowance must be made in an interpretation of the statistics is that colored imbeciles are frequently classified as criminals. In the South very little provision is made for the demented Negro. He is allowed to run wild until the commission of some serious crime brings him within the reach of the law, and then he is classified as a criminal. In the North similar conditions persist because officials do not wish to assign colored individuals to white asylums. Reuter states that there are only a few hundred feeble-minded colored children in special institutions.[18]

Another extrinsic factor of much greater importance is the condition of the colored home. A distinguished psychologist has written: "The time for socializing the fundamental activities is childhood, and the place for doing it is the home. In post adolescent years or in later childhood the inhibitions of anti-social trends and the formation of socialized habits become almost impossible. The reason why the Negro tends to be anti-social is that growing up in an environment of poverty and ignorance where stealth and depredation are often the accepted means of livelihood, he has had no opportunity for developing socialized traits. . . . The aim therefore should be not for more education but earlier education. We need not so much colleges for members of the colored race as homes in which they can be properly reared."[19]

---

17 "The Negro in Detroit," sec. IX, p. 9.

18 Op. cit., p. 361. Cf. Woofter, "The Basis of Racial Adjustment," p. 128.

19 Allport, "Social Psychology," p. 387.

The first requisite for the development of home life among any people is that the mother be in the home a greater part of the day. In the slave period the colored women left their homes early in the morning and remained away until evening. The practice, though declining, has continued among the Negro group until the present time. According to the census of 1920, approximately forty per cent of the Negro women were gainfully employed, whereas only seventeen per cent of the white women were so engaged. Many colored children are thus deprived of essential moral training. When the parents are away the children take to the streets, where they come in contact with moral degenerates and acquire familiarity with all the vices and vulgarities. The moral life of many colored families in the North is further jeopardized by the presence of lodgers. The difficulty of finding a home adequate for a family of four or five persons has forced many Negroes to take over large buildings in better locations at a high rent. To meet the difficulty of paying the rent lodgers are taken in. The Detroit Race Commission reported, "Overcrowding with the resulting lack of privacy which frequently makes members of both sexes occupy the same room and the presence in the population of a majority of men are factors responsible for the large number of sexual crimes."[20]

The poor quality of religious instruction which many Negroes receive may explain some of the crime. After emancipation the Negroes tended to withdraw within themselves. In accordance with that movement they founded their own churches and selected ministers from their own race. Those ministers, unfortunately, with few exceptions were not equipped either mentally or morally for such leadership. Less than twenty years ago a Negro minister wrote of the religious leaders of his denomination: "To be sure, there were good ministers among them—men of sterling qualities—but these were in the minority and were paid little attention to.

20 "The Negro in Detroit," sec. IX, p. 16.

The majority of the ministers were sadly lacking in education . . . .. When I added their mental unpreparedness to their unlovely personal traits I could not see in them enough of these better qualifications which fit men for a holy calling or for leadership.''[21] The Detroit Commission observed: ''The fact that there are such a limited number of capable ministers in such a large church membership as Detroit's Negro community possesses, presents a very pathetic situation. Not more than ten per cent of the forty-four pastors of the leading and reputable churches are graduates of high schools—that type of individual is a liability rather than an asset.''[22]

Consequently in addition to the evil habits which the Negro acquired during slavery, there exist today many external factors which must inevitably foster criminals among the colored group:—the presence of disorderly houses in their residential districts, deplorable home conditions, defective religious teaching, difficulty in securing employment, inadequate recreational facilities.[23] Those forces when accumulated seem to provide sufficient explanation for the prevalency of crime among the colored group. There is no need of postulating an innate criminal tendency.

Some white people while recognizing environment as an explanation for much of the Negro's crime insist that several immoral tendencies of the Negro are definitely natural. One such tendency is that manifested by many colored domestics who steal and pilfer small articles from their employers. Yet the mental attitudes acquired by the race during slavery seem to offer a sufficient explanation for that weakness. Jefferson adverted to the tendency in his day and thought the disposition to theft with which the Negro has been branded must be ascribed

21 Corrothers, ''In Spite of the Handicap,'' p. 168.
22 Op. cit., sec. X, p. 16.
23 Cf. ''The Negro in Chicago,'' p. 341; and *The Annals*, vol. 98, p. 217.

to his situation and not to any depravity of the moral sense. Mrs. Hammond, a Southern woman, attributes the persistence of the trait even among well-paid domestics to the indifference and the connivance of their employers. "I and others like me," she writes, "have been training her and ten thousand more to shiftlessness and dishonesty ever since they were born. The wonder is not that so many of them are worthless but that there are so many honest, painstaking, trustworthy ones among us."[24]

The numerous sexual offenses of colored women are attributed by some white individuals to an innate weakness rather than environment. Yet Dr. Ruth Reed in her study of Negro Illegitimacy found that in 500 cases of unmarried colored mothers there was a notable lack of home influence. So she concluded, "there is no conclusive evidence that Negro women are meeting the problem of family life in any way which may be regarded as characteristically racial."[25] Dowd, a Southerner, has written: "In rural communities, especially among the property owning class, there are thousands of married Negro women whose fidelity is above suspicion, and in all the cities, especially among the home owning class who are able to separate themselves from the slum influence, there are young girls and mothers whose chastity is untainted."[26] Indeed, there is an abundance of testimony given by priests and others who have labored among the colored people that not only the Negro women but the men and the children when given the opportunities for religious training and when placed in a wholesome environment compare very favorably with the whites.[27]

---

24 Hammond, "In Black and White," p. 86.
25 Reed, "Negro Illegitimacy in New York City," p. 132.
26 Dowd, op. cit., p. 100.
27 *America*, vol. 26, pp. 468, 564, 565. *Fortnightly Review*, Jan. 15, 1925, p. 27.

The Incorrigibility of Race Friction

Jefferson wrote in 1820; "Nothing is more certainly written in the book of fate than that these people are to be free; nor is it less certain than that the two races equally free cannot live in the same government." The first of these two prophecies has certainly been realized. Some Americans think sufficient evidence exists to prove the second. Believing that the white man's repugnance or prejudice against the Negro is insurmountable, many Christians in the United States hold that each racial group will realize its highest happiness only when they are separated. Consequently those individuals do not interest themselves in the Negro group. Apathetically they are awaiting some practical scheme of expatriation.

The prejudice will undoubtedly persist as a serious factor for generations. Yet it is not an inseparable element in the association of blacks and whites. Data will be presented in the next chapter which indicate that race prejudice is not an instinctive but an acquired reaction. In subsequent generations, as the Negro acquires education, refinement, wealth and greater self-control, the attitude of the whites may change.

It is, also, interesting to note that in some other lands the feeling against the Negro is not as intense. Of the first Negroes introduced into Portugal the court chronicler wrote: "While some of the captives were not able to endure the change and died happily as Christians, the others, dispersed among Portuguese households, so ingratiated themselves that they were set free and some were married to men and women of the land and acquired comfortable estates."[28] The modern European entertains very little prejudice. In Jamaica, "There is no artificial or conventional disqualification whatever to bar any Jamaican of Negro or mixed race from occupying any position for which he is intellectually qualified in any department of the social life of the island, including

---

28 Phillips, "American Negro Slavery," p. 2.

the public service."[29] The same statement could accurately be applied to Cuba and to Brazil.[30]

Consequently, Lord Bryce has written: "Instead of being, as we Teutonic people are apt to assume, the rule in the matter we are rather the exception, for in the ancient world there seems to have been little race repulsion; there is very little today among Mohammedans; there is none among the Chinese.—This seems to suggest that since the phenomenon is not of the essence of human nature it may not be always as strong among the Teutonic people as it is today. Religion has been in the past almost as powerful as a dissevering force as has racial antagonism. In the case of the Spaniards and Portuguese religion made race differences seem insignificant."[31]

In the social life of the United States there may be found evidence of the working of forces which should ultimately improve the relations between the black and the white races. One force, essentially economic, is represented in the spectacular migrations of the Southern Negroes to the Northern States. Between 1910 and 1924 approximately 600,000 Negroes moved northward.[32] These migrations were occasioned principally by the shortage of labor in the industrial plants of the North and by the failure of the crops in the South. Probably they were but a disproportionate shadow of a smaller but consistent movement of the Negroes from those districts of the South in which they have been oppressed. The shortage of labor occasioned by the restrictions upon European immigration should draw the Negroes westward and northward.

One effect of the migrations is the diminution of the Southern hatred and prejudice against the Negro. The

---

29 Olivier, "White Capital and Colored Labour," p. 34.
30 Reuter, "The Mulatto in the United States," p. 59.
31 Bryce, "South American Observations and Impressions," p. 477. Cf. Bennett, "Forty Years in Brazil," pp. 60-65. Cf. Junod, II, "L'attitude des Peuples Latin vis-a-vis des Races de Color," in *The Student World*, July, 1926, p. 139.
32 "Negro Year Book," p. 6.

fear of black domination has always deeply influenced the average Southerner and has motivated many acts of hostility. Naturally the departure of thousands of the colored race should lessen that fear. "Destroy once for all," writes Tannenbaum, "the fear of Negro preponderance and the practice of Negro baiting, Negro hatred, and Negro complex will go simmering by the board."[33] The exodus has, also, occasioned in some sections of the South a shortage of labor. That shortage has forced the Southerner to recognize that the Negro had been a valuable asset to the community. In fact, in some localities, earnest efforts were made to keep the Negro. Occasionally they assumed the form of excessively burdensome regulations for Northern labor agents. More frequently they were evidenced in an attempt to provide better schools and better police protection for the colored group.

The sudden influx of such a large number of Negroes into the cities of the North occasioned considerable friction. But much of that friction was temporary and has abated. Of New York City whose colored population increased 66.3 per cent between 1910 and 1920, James Weldon Johnson, a Negro, has written: "On the whole I know of no place in the country where the feeling is so cordial and at the same time so matter-of-fact and taken for granted."[34] In Detroit, which may be regarded as a typical industrial city, thousands of Negroes have secured employment. Yet the peace of the community has not been gravely disturbed. The Mayor's Race Commission declared, "Employers were unanimous in stating that they had no more clashes in their plants between Negroes and whites than between groups of white workers and other nationalities."[35] Certainly, if race contacts are viewed nationally, the net result of the dispersion of the colored group is the diminution of race prejudice. The migrations have transformed race prejudice from a sectional to a national factor. Though the preju-

33 Op. cit., p. 166.
34 Locke, "The New Negro," p. 311.
35 Op. cit., sec. III, p. 29. Cf. *Annals*, vol. 98, p. 214.

dice has been scattered, its intensity has been weakened.

Besides economic forces there are numerous agencies working valiantly and heroically for the improvement of race relations. In both the North and in the South the various religious agencies have finally recognized the racial conflict as a moral issue and are concentrating their resources for an attack upon the problem. Information is being collected and published relative to the arbitrary character of prejudice and the cultural achievements of the Negro. In the Sunday Schools and religious classes an effort is being made to correlate the practice of the virtues of charity and justice with racial contacts. A detailed list of those activities will be found in the ninth chapter.

In addition to religious bodies there are numerous social organizations which are concerned about improving the material conditions of the colored group and hence indirectly about the elimination of prejudice. Of these organizations, one deserving of special attention is the National Urban League which "aims to adjust the Negro to an urban environment." Through campaigns conducted by the League in the larger cities, many of the colored have been encouraged to improve and beautify their homes. During these campaigns the interest of municipal authorities was often won and a more extensive enforcement of sanitary laws in colored districts has been secured. It was through the influence of the League that Rockefeller was induced to spend several millions for new apartment houses for the colored in New York City. Through the Industrial Department of the League efforts have been made to guarantee positions for the colored in the large factories. Because the applicants recommended by the League were graded and examined the co-operation of the employers was easily gained and a favorable opinion about the value of colored labor was secured. During the year 1920, over 15,000 Negroes were placed in Chicago alone. Through the administration department an effort is made to give white people a keener understanding of the progress being made by the colored group. Interracial meetings are held for the frank discussion of mutual problems, and reporters and representatives of welfare organizations are taken frequently on tours through the Negro districts. An indication of the extensiveness of the League's work is the fact that during the year 1926 over $400,000 was raised and expended.[36]

In the South there exist, also, organizations consecrated to the improvement of race relationships. The University Commission on Southern Race Problems, an organization composed of University professors, meets from time to time to study various phases of the race question. The Commission by its open letters to the college students of the South has changed considerably the public opinion of the section.

But the most influential organization is the Commission on Interracial Co-operation. After the armistice, an effort was made by white leaders to form committees which would help both the white and the colored soldier to make the necessary post-war adjustments and to improve relationships between the races, which had grown strongly antagonistic. Ten-day schools were formed for the study of community readjustments and the funds for the work were furnished by the War council of the Y. M. C. A. In that movement the Commission had its origin. The executive board of the Commission from the headquarters at Atlanta, Georgia, is entrusted with the task of organizing state committees, which are composed of prominent Negroes and whites and which have two paid secretaries. Those committees are expected to concern themselves about the protection of the rights of the colored in state institutions. The secretaries are obliged to strive to organize county interracial committees which would interest themselves in local problems such as gaining justice in lower courts and repressing mobs. Over 800 county interracial committees have been organized, and they are functioning effectively. For example, an appropriation of over one million dollars was recently

---

36 *Opportunity*, March, 1927.

secured for the colored schools in Atlanta; the colored hospital was greatly improved in Savannah, and an efficient legal aid society was organized in Nashville.[37]

Throughout many parts of the South, a growing conviction has developed, that the Negro should be treated more equitably. The fruit which such a conviction may bear in the future is exemplified in the conditions existing at the present time in Durham, North Carolina. The 8,000 Negroes in that town constitute one-third of the total population. Yet, according to the statement of a prominent colored business man, they live "on peaceful and friendly terms with their white neighbors. They find employment in tobacco factories and hosiery mills; the vote is not denied because of color; adequate educational opportunities are provided and they receive an honest hearing in the courts."[38] Another instance of the same spirit was manifested in the reception accorded to James Weldon Johnson, a Negro poet, when, during the Institute of Human Relations week of 1927, he lectured and held seminar courses in the University of North Carolina. The "Tar Heeler," the student publication, recorded the event with pride and contrasted Johnson with the famous poet slave of North Carolina, Horton. "Horton's position was that of the bended knee. James Weldon Johnson has come with the majesty of an exalted leader."[39]

The mere institution of organizations such as the National Urban League or the Commission on Interracial Co-operation does not constitute a solution for the race problem. Yet, if their efforts are combined with other factors—such as the northern migrations, the relative character of prejudice, the material and the cultural development of the Negro, the satisfactory adjustments made by a few pioneers—they give indications of the improbability of the contention that both races cannot live together peacefully and happily.

---

37 Woofter, op. cit., p. 34.
38 Cf. Speer, "Race and Race Relations," p. 324.
39 *Opportunity*, June, 1927, p. 181.

The Extinction of the Negro

Orestes Brownson prophesied, at the end of the Civil War, that after a few generations the Negro would cease to constitute a problem for the United States. The solution would come by the extinction of the Negro race. Deprived of the protection of the slave-holder and the sanitary regulations of the plantations, the colored race, being a weaker race, would be unable to withstand the rugged climate and the ravages of disease. Forty years later, Hoffman, a statistician for an insurance company, made a similar prophecy. In 1927, Professor Frank H. Hankins, of Smith College, declared: "By 1935, according to present indications, I believe the Negro population of the United States will be decreasing absolutely, and I think that this will go on until as a separate population the Negro will have ceased to be a factor of importance."[40] That such an event will occur is undoubtedly the secret wish of many white people. But it is not immediately probable. However, consideration must be given to the contention because some people are so impressed by the wish that they think little and do less about improving present-day racial relations.

The Negroes constitute a smaller proportion of the population of the United States today than at any time during the last one hundred and thirty years. In 1790 they comprised 19 per cent of the total population; in 1860, 14 per cent, and in 1920, 9.9 per cent. That fact itself, though, does not necessarily *imply* the extinction of the population because the increase of the white group has been due to extensive migrations from Europe. Actually, the colored population has grown greatly, and the increase has been to a large extent a natural one. During the slave period the increase was at the rate of two per cent annually. Since 1870, the colored group has more than doubled itself.

Yet there are two other facts which might augur seriously for the future of the colored group. One is the

---

40 *New York Times,* Sunday, March, 20, 1927.

exceptionally sharp drop in the colored rate of increase during the decade ending in 1920. For that decade the rate of increase was only 6.5 per cent for the colored, while for the preceding decade it was 16 per cent. However, that sharp decline may be due to the exceptional conditions of the period. A similar condition prevailed in the decade ending in 1870 when the per cent of increase dropped from 22.1 to 9.9. Both periods were for the Negro epochs of great social and economic change. The decade between 1910 and 1920 was practically that of a second emancipation. Possibly because of the extensive movement within the colored group, many Negroes were not enumerated by the census officials.[41] The other fact is the rise of the death rate among the colored population to the point that in many cities the deaths are greater in number than the births. That condition, also, is probably temporary and may be due to the congested and unsanitary areas into which large numbers of the Negroes have been segregated.

At present strenuous efforts are being made to reduce the death rate, and they are meeting with considerable success. Many of the diseases which have been reaping heavy tolls among the colored are rapidly being brought under control. Tuberculosis was in 1910 the cause of one-fifth of their deaths. But between 1910 and 1922 the death rate from that disease was reduced by 42 per cent.[42] The mortality rate for Negro children has declined so that now it corresponds to that of the whites for 1911. The Negro death rate will, also, be greatly reduced by the growing consciousness among the whites of the inseparable relation existing between the health conditions of both races. Germs know no color line.

Scientists have disputed whether the high death rate of the Negro in the city is attributable entirely to environment or whether it is due in some measure to hereditary factors. While the point has not been settled there is, however, no strong justification for the contention

---

41 "Negro Year Book," p. 422.
42 "Negro Year Book," pp. 404-412.

that the colored group in the United States will become extinct. Dr. Louis J. Dublin, statistician for the Metropolitan Life Insurance Company writes, "The doleful prophecies of those who saw the race problem solved through his extinction have been absolutely discredited by recent events."[43] James A. Tobey, former administrative Secretary of the National Health Council and a member of the staff of the Massachusetts Institute of Technology, states: "Considered dispassionately, therefore, it seems likely that the nearly eleven million Negroes in this country will not eventually die out but will continue for many years to come to be a significant element in our social structure and one of our civic and national problems."[44]

The greater part of this chapter has been devoted to an examination of contentions, such as the alleged inferiority of the Negro, upon which radical proposals for the solution of the race problem have been based. They were examined not because the proposals have any importance but because the same contentions are regarded as justification for attitudes, which though less radical, affect the Negro deeply. In regard to the solution of the American Negro Problem it seems too clear for extended argument that there is no patent magic solution. The Negro is here and here for good. The races will continue to live side by side while adjustments are slowly made which will make life most tolerable for the Negro. Toward those Negroes every white American has numerous duties and obligations,—obligations which have been neglected in the past. The examination and definition of those duties and obligations will occupy our attention in subsequent chapters.

---

43 *American Mercury,* Sept., 1927, p. 41.
44 *Current History,* Nov., 1926, p. 220.

CHAPTER III

BASIC PRINCIPLES

Before the captain of a coastwise vessel takes his ship from port he always studies well the lights, the buoys, and the landmarks of the territory through which his prospective course will take him. Likewise, before setting out into a detailed discussion of the morality of intricate discriminations it is advisable that we review several important moral principles. Possibly to some these principles may appear as obvious as platitudes. Yet earnest examination of them must be made because they are the lights, the buoys by which the course of the discussion must be guided.

The Negro as a Subject of Rights

According to Christian teaching, rights in the moral sense of the term are usually defined as inviolable moral claims to personal goods. Since they are almost as extensive as human needs, there are many species of rights and many divisions. But the division most pertinent to this discussion is that of their separation into natural and civil rights. Natural rights are those which a man acquires with his nature, and they are designed as means for attaining his natural end. They are so indigenous that no human power, not even the State, can abrogate them. The State, however, may determine their limits and extension. Civil rights, on the other hand, are bestowed by the State for a civil purpose. In the distribution of civil rights, the State enjoys considerable power. Some rights, if the common good so demands, may be restricted to certain classes of citizens and may be abrogated by the State if they have already been bestowed. However, there are many other types of civil rights which the State cannot annul and which must be bestowed upon all the inhabitants. They are but formal expressions of natural rights.

The fountain head in which natural rights have their source and justification is the end of man. That end, according to the perennial teaching of the Church of Christ, is immediately and exclusively the glorification of God. Each human individual was created to glorify God formally by adoration and objectively by living according to his nature. Thus the Creator's great work is manifested. "To live according to his nature," implies the proportionate development of the distinctively human faculties, the intellect and the will, and the proportionate subjugation of the lower faculties. It means that moral and reasonable living which is expected of all men because of their rational nature and end. In that destination of all men to the objective and formal glorification of God there is to be found, as Bouquillon observed in his study of the foundation of Christian morals, "Not only the source of obligations but even the most firm foundation of the dignity, the independence, the liberty, and the rights of the individual man to life and property."[1] Because if man is bound to glorify God by leading a moral and reasonable life the Divine Creator must have bestowed upon him the moral faculty of using means necessary to the attainment of that end. Those means are the natural rights, the inviolable moral powers of performing certain actions, of possessing certain goods; and they are so sacred that all persons except those in whom they reside are morally restrained from interfering with them. In addition to the physical powers by which man lives, as a human being, he needs those moral inviolable powers without which his end cannot be obtained.

In the United States natural rights are frequently designated and summarized as the rights to life, liberty, and property. But if such a summary is accepted those

---

1 Bouquillon, "Theologia Moralis Fundamentalis," p. 149.

terms must be interpreted very widely. Life must include immunity from all forms of physical assault. Liberty must extend beyond mere physical movement to the fields of education, religion, and employment. As a theologian has recently observed, "Natural rights include all those moral powers, opportunities, and immunities which the individual requires in order to obtain the end of his nature, to live a reasonable life."[2]

The complement of that Christian teaching is the doctrine that all men are essentially equal and consequently have equal natural rights. All men, cultured and savage, belong to the same species of being and have in Adam a common Father to whom the words were spoken, "Fill the earth and subdue it and rule over the fishes of the sea and the fowls of the air and all living creatures which move upon the earth." All men have essentially similar natures. All men radically are rational, self-active, independent beings, complete in themselves. No man is a mere instrument, as an animal, to the convenience of another. All men have the same end to obtain, and consequently they have equal claims to the essentials necessary to its acquisition. As Pope Leo observed, "No man may outrage with impunity the human dignity which God Himself treats with reverence or stand in the way of that higher life which is the preparation for the eternal life of heaven."[3] Hence since their natures and ends are identical, all men must be of equal intrinsic worth and their natural rights which are necessary to the attainment of that end must be equal.

If this fundamental doctrine of Christianity is applied to the American Race Problem, the white Christian must admit that the natural rights of a Negro are identical in number and sacredness with the natural rights of the white man. No matter how strong the prejudice, no matter how consistently throughout history he may have been regarded as the hewer of wood and the drawer of water, his natural rights must be respected

---

2 Ryan, "The State and the Church," p. 225.
3 Encyclical Letter, "Rerum Novarum."

as these of the white man. For, natural rights are rooted not upon membership in one nation or upon membership in the white race but upon the sacredness which the individual enjoys because of his end. As a distinguished matron of the South has observed, "Everybody on earth is human first and racial afterwards. We must see in the Negro first of all, deeper than all, higher than all, the man made in the image of God as truly as ourselves."[4] If it is a crime and a wrong to destroy the life of a white man, or arbitrarily to suppress his development, or to mutilate his body, the same act when perpetrated against the Negro is equally wrong. Indeed, the only Christian who can logically hold that the Negro's essential rights, such as the right to life, are inferior to those of the white man is the person holding the thesis that the Negro is not a man but a member of some inferior species of being, intermediate between animals and men.

No sane person explicitly maintains that the Negro is not a man or that his life is less sacred than that of a white man. But many white Christians are, in their daily actions, influenced by a conviction that the Negro's rights to certain goods such as property, education, and industrial opportunities are secondary to those of white men. A partial explanation for that conviction is to be found in the persistency of a tradition that the Negroes being the descendants of Chanaan, the son Cham, are cursed by God, that their color, their enslavement in past generations, and their menial condition in the present generation, are evidences of the curse. The tradition is, of course, false and originated in the minds of the slave holding class who were seeking a moral justification for the institution. But since many students in Christian colleges give evidence of having accepted the tradition as a doctrine of orthodox Christianity, it may be advisable to state that there is no evidence that the Negroes are the descendants of Chanaan. The reason for the absence of evidence is that all the descendants of

---

[4] Hammond, "In Black and White," p. 88.

Chanaan were either killed by the Israelites or perished in the downfall of Phoenicia.[5] Moreover, to construe their mental condition as evidence that they are accursed by God is a dangerous mental process. By the same process of reasoning a large number of white Christians throughout the world, might be proved accursed.

Another fact which has contributed to the adoption of such a mental attitude is that the white race in the United States has been deeply impressed by the relatively tardy development of the Negro and the weaknesses of the colored group. They, like their forebears, have yielded to an insidious force which has even altered systems of philosophy. Professor A. J. Carlyle, holds that during the fourteenth and fifteenth centuries the discovery of primitive tribes in Africa and America occasioned a revival of the notion of the essential inequality of the human races which had disappeared from post-Aristotolian philosophy and the theology of Christianity.[6] The white race in America has been so strongly influenced by the differences that many white individuals, while admitting the equality of all men and races as an abstract theory, believe for most practical purposes that the rights of the white man and the Negro are as unequal as are the white and Negro races. That opinion, though defective, reflects the shadow of a great truth and suggests the necessity of indicating the relation between the Christian doctrine of the equal rights of all men and the Christian doctrine of proportional justice.

Within the white race men differ greatly one from the other. One man possesses the ability which distinguishes him as a great surgeon and another can sacrcely absorb elementary school subjects. Some people are born with an executive talent and others find their happiness in obedience. Obviously, the man who lacks the proper qualifications has no right to an elaborate university education or to an executive position in a

---

5 Cf. Father Haas' article, "The Negroes and the Curse of Chanaan," *Our Colored Missions*, Nov., 1927, p. 164.

6 Cf. Marvin, "Western Races and The World," p. 119.

large industrial plant. For proportional justice and the canon of human welfare require, as Christian teachers have always insisted, that individuals endowed with different powers should be given correspondingly different positions and different amounts of goods. Nature has made men in some respects very unequal, and it seems absolutely equitable that in those respects they should be treated unequally.[7]

Though allowances must be made for the differences and inequalities which actually exist among men there is a minimum of goods which all men both black and white need and upon which all have a claim. That minimum is determined by the sacredness of the human individual and by the reasonable needs of the human personality. It involves all negative rights and a reasonable immunity from encroachments upon personal liberty. It involves in return for honest labor, remuneration sufficient to maintain a worker and his family in normal health and comfort. That minimum includes, also, opportunities for recreation, education, and church membership, and an opportunity to secure a home in an environment which safeguard morality. To all those goods the rights of all men both black and white are equal. To deny a Negro less is to degrade him, to treat him as an animal.

The rights of men to more than the conventional minimum are dependent upon their peculiar needs, capacities, efforts, abilities, and must be regulated by proportional justice. Consequently, it has been well said that, "the rights of all men are equal in number, kind, and sacredness but not in quantity or absolute content." But it should be noted that the right to more than the minimum is based upon the ability and the efforts of the individual and not to any considerable extent upon membership in a certain family or race.[8]

People of this generation look askance at any system in which the goods above the minimum and the posi-

---

7 Taparelli, "Droit Naturel," p. 354.
8 Ryan, "Distributive Justice," p. 260.

tions of trust in the industrial and commercial life of a community are distributed only upon the basis of family or racial association. And properly so. Unless the necessity of such a distribution to the common good can be proved, a double injustice may be involved. Judging by the experience of past ages it seems most probable that some individuals in the so-called lower classes possess ability greater than that possessed by the members of the favored families who often hold the more desirable positions. Thus in some general way proportionate justice is violated. Furthermore, the injection of family relationships as an indispensable condition of advance violates the right of opportunity, the right to be free from unreasonable interference when in pursuit of any lawful good. Theologians vindicate that right to the individual because the contrary, the arbitrary denial of an opportunity for progress, renders men bitter, resentful, morose, and destroys the happiness and contentment which is necessary for reasonable living. To deny progress and development to all except those born in a certain family or race is a most arbitrary restriction.

When these statements are applied to the Negro problem in this country it follows that the Negro just as the white man has a claim to goods above the minimum proportionate to his abilities and efforts. Or more practically the Negro has the right of opportunity, the right to be free from arbitrary interference. Nor is the objection pertinent that the Negroes as a group are retarded or inferior. Even if the inferiority of the group is admitted there exists, as all psychologists admit, considerable overlapping. Unquestionably some Negroes possess talent greater than that possessed by the average white. Color is not an accurate or reliable basis for the measurement of ability. "The ethical attitude to assume toward the relation of races is, therefore, one which recognizes the worth and merit of individual personalities wherever they are found."[9]

The natural rights which an individual potentially possesses become actual in the concrete circumstances in which the vicissitudes of life place him. The American Negro is neither a State ward nor is he a subject for expatriation. Legally he is a subject of the United States. Consequently his natural rights as outlined above become actual in the existing phases of American life. In subsequent chapters an inquiry will be made into the extent and the specific interpretation of some of those rights.

Thus far the discussion has been limited to an examination of the natural rights of the Negro. There is however another group of rights, civil rights, which are conferred by the State in its own interest. When a civil right has been validly bestowed it is as sacred and as inviolable as a natural right. Any infringement upon a civil right is as much a crime as the violation of the right which an individual receives from nature or from a personal contract.

The United States Government confers upon the Negro who was born within its domains or who has been duly naturalized the full citizenship of the United States and of the State in which he resides. Upon such a Negro are bestowed all the immunities, privileges, and opportunities which any white citizen enjoys. Hence, since every act of a government is presumed to be a valid exercise of its power, every civil right which the Negro legally possesses must be regarded as valid unless the contrary in a particular instance has been clearly proved. The violation of such a right is an injustice. The seriousness of the injustice is to be gauged by the importance of the right relative both to the individual Negro and to the colored group. In later chapters specific violations will be discussed in detail.

---

9 Woofter, "The Basis of Racial Adjustment," p. 12.

The Negro and Christian Charity

"Thou shalt love thy neighbor as thyself," is a fundamental and distinctively Christian precept. It is, also, an accepted Christian dogma that the word neighbor is a synonym for all mankind; that the Christian is obliged to love each and every human being irrespective of class, race, color, sex, or age. By deduction or implication white individuals are forced to admit that the commandment extends to the Negro. Frequently throughout the ages the Christian Church has transformed that belief into action. Recently a most striking evidence of the Church's conviction was manifested in the beatification of the twenty-two Negro martyrs of Uganda on the same day that Joan of Arc was canonized.

The acknowledgment must be made that many Christians in the United States, although assenting in theory to the proposition, have failed to show in their daily lives any love for the Negro. The fruits of love—courtesy, respect, kindness, and mercy—have been limited to their own race. White Christians ensnared by the world-wide tendency to adopt a double standard of morality have limited the practice of Christian charity to men of their own color. The failure of some is traceable partly to the absence of any consciousness of an obligation to treat the Negro charitably. And that absence, in turn, is due to the negligence of Christian teachers. The failure of others is attributable to discouragement occasioned by an exaggerated interpretation of the commandment by humanitarians. Yet it is, also, true that wholesome actions of white Christians have at times been designated as violations of the commandment by unbelievers who completely misunderstood the words of Christ. In the following paragraphs, then, there may appropriately be undertaken an examination of the actions which are rendered obligatory toward the Negro by the commandment, "Thou shalt love thy neighbor as thyself."

Christian charity does not impose any obligation of blinding oneself to the differences existing between the black and white races in America, to the dissimilarity of physical features, of temperament, of culture. But the Christian while confronted by those realities is obliged to recognize another truth which, though not self-evident, is just as real; namely, that the Negro being a rational creature is capable of obtaining eternal happiness, is made to the image of God, and was redeemed by Christ. The white individual is obliged to love the Negro, not because of his swarthy color, but because of his relation to God, because he is loved by God, because: "The Lord, both of them and of you, is in heaven and there is no respect of persons with Him."

The obligation of loving the Negro has appeared discouragingly arduous or repulsive to many whites because of their exaggerated notions of the meaning of the commandment. Many people have mistakenly thought that Christian love for one's neighbor implied necessarily a feeling of affection for him, a feeling similar to that felt for a blood relative. On the contrary such feelings being to a considerable extent uncontrollable are but accidents to love. Love in its essence is an act of the will, a choice, a determination to show concern for and interest in another.

A belief has flourished that Christian love of neighbor implies an obligation constantly to subordinate personal needs and personal happiness for the sake of another. But such actions, though frequently evidences of heroic and generous love are not obligatory. Man's love for his neighbor need not always equal his love of self. The Christian is commended only to love his neighbor *as* himself. The authoritative teaching of Christianity on this matter was summarized by St. Thomas Aquinas centuries ago in the expression, "Man's love for himself is the model of his love for another."[10] In his inner thoughts and feelings a man naturally and primarily wishes happiness to himself and kin and Christ did not change that fundamental law. But he did forbid his

---

10 "Summa Theologica," 2a, 2ae, q. 24, a. 4.

disciples to confine their love to self and family. He commanded them to love all mankind. That good-will toward mankind, however, need not be as passionate or as intense as love of self or kin, since man is attracted to self and kin by natural bonds. Moreover, in the external pursuit of happiness a man is generally permitted to seek first those objects which are reasonably necessary for the welfare of self and family, only secondly need he concern himself about the happiness of others.[11]

What actions, then, are rendered obligatory by the great commandment of love? In regard to internal actions Christian teachers have always insisted that the precept implied wishing a neighbor well, rejoicing over his happiness, sorrowing over his misfortunes, and resolving to give assistance to the needy if this could be done without great inconvenience.[12] Obviously, however, the Divine law does not impose the impossible duty of entertaining such thoughts about each and every individual. Rather the obligation is generally satisfied by a feeling of good-will toward all mankind including the Negro race. But the duty of entertaining charitable thoughts toward all men is violated by acquiescence in hateful feelings toward any individual or race. Hence the familiar unbalanced hatred of the Negro race and its individual members is sinful. The failure to repress or to attempt to control prejudice and antipathy against the Negro is just as wrong as the neglect to attempt the repression of the passion of anger or of sloth. From such unbridled prejudices have been born serious injustices.

In respect to external actions a man is obviously not bound to journey constantly about scattering favors. The external application of the commandment is confined largely to those contracts which are occasioned by the daily fulfilment of duties. The external application is summarized in the old adage, "What you wish done

---

11 Op. cit., 2a, 2ae, q. 26, art. 3.
12 Noldin, "Summa Theologiae Moralis," vol II, p. 87.

to yourself do to another."[13] At all times there is an obligation of restraining any word or deed which could reasonably offend or harm another. Hence to address a colored person with such terms as "nigger" or "coon," or to use any epithet which implies opprobrium is wrong. To mock, to insult, or to perform any action which implies disdain is sinful, for they are the antitheses of love. Usually the same civilities and politenesses shown to white man should also be manifested to the Negro. The custom of treating him only as an inferior prevails in many sections. Such a practice may have been defensible during the slave period. To a limited extent it is permissible today toward colored domestics since white servants are treated in a similar manner. Yet it is difficult to find any reason which would justify the extension of the practice to strangers especially since the number of refined and cultured Negroes is constantly increasing. Such an attitude may not have offended the slave but it does offend the modern Negro, and many members of the white race, especially those associated with the Interracial Commission are abandoning the practice. However in the failure of white men to invite Negroes to their homes there is no uncharitableness involved, for no man has a claim to such a courtesy. That and other actions of the same type constitute marks of special friendship and they are due to no man. As Aquinas taught centuries ago, "Outside of cases of urgency to show such favors belongs to the perfection of charity."[14]

Besides refraining from offensive actions every man is bound to aid the needy from his abundance or surplus. But, except in cases of extreme need, this obligation becomes pressing only when the reasonable needs of the individual and of his family have been satisfied.[15] Some Americans have the practice of giving generously to the needy in Oriental or European lands and of completely

13 Cathrein, "Philosophia Moralis," p. 238.
14 Op. cit., 2a., 2ae.. q. 25.
15 Lehmkuhl, "Theologia Moralis," vol. I, p. 418.

neglecting the Negro. Such a practice is wrong. The Christian rule of distribution has been thus described by St. Augustine: "Since one cannot do good to all we ought to consider those chiefly who by reason of place, time, or any other circumstance, or by a kind of chance are more closely united to us."[16] Since the Negro is a resident of the same country he has prior claim upon the white man's charity.

In the matter of giving alms to the needy Negroes in the form of goods or clothing the white people of the South are above reproach. Other wants of the colored people, however, have not been so well provided for. Negroes who belong to the Catholic communion have a dire need of schools and churches. The entire colored population needs better homes, instruction from social workers in the care of the home, and guidance in the selection of work as they come North. The satisfaction of those multitudinous wants are works of mercy, and every white individual is under some obligation to make provision for them from his abundance. Since those exigences are dominantly social they can be best satisfied by the work of elaborate social organizations such as the National Urban League. Christians should contribute to the support of such organizations. Father La Farge has observed: "If we are not all to drift down together into a Dead Sea sterile of hope and charity let us join with those within and without the Church who are trying to remedy the Negro's condition."[17]

Americans, also, frequently restrict the scope of mercy to the donation of food, clothing, and shelter. Yet Christian writers have always insisted upon giving the commandment a wider meaning and have taught that it includes an obligation both of preventing evil from befalling a neighbor and also of restraining any action which might harm him. Otherwise the love of one's neighbor is scarcely genuine. Today the source from which many of the Negro's miseries flow is race prej-

---

16 Cf. Aquinas, op. cit., 2a., 2ae., q. 26, a. 6.
17 *America,* March 5, 1927, p. 604.

udice, the prejudice which bars to him the door of opportunity. This prejudice is to a large extent organic and deeply rooted. Yet many Christians during the course of a year are placed in situations in which by an action or by a word they could, without serious inconvenience, modify slightly that prejudice. It seems that they are under some obligation to do so.

An effort has been made here to delineate merely the actions which are rendered absolutely obligatory by the great commandment of love; to delineate the minimum number of actions which a Christian may perform without violating the commandment. Such a minimum is obviously not the standard or the ideal of the fervent Christian. True love is all embracing. In proportion as the individual strives to grow to the stature of Christ and in proportion as the intensity of his love increases, he will endeavor to perform many other acts of service and kindness toward the colored group. For the purse of charity is never empty, the measure of charity is never filled, and the patience of charity is never exhausted. Even to list these supererogatory actions would be impossible since the simple law of charity cannot be codified on the earth.

However, it may be helpful to advert to several fields of activity in which genuine acts of Christian charity might be performed. White individuals have thought themselves very benevolent if they gave their colored domestics old clothing or unused food. But they would perform an invaluable act of charity if they would assist their domestics to secure an attractive home in an environment and neighborhood in which the moral life of both parents and children would enjoy some protection. Fraternal and charitable associations such as the Knights of Columbus could co-operate with colored leaders in an effort to secure from the municipal authorities equitable enforcement of police regulations and of sanitary laws in the colored districts. School teachers would perform a work most acceptable to Christ if they endeavored by an occasional suggestion or illustration to diminish the racial prejudice of children. Such works would not only be helpful to the Negro but would have special merit because the Divine Master proclaimed, "As long as you do it to one of these, my least brethren, you do it to me."

Race Prejudice and Its Moral Implications

Thus far in the review of the principles and factors which must enter into every moral judgment on the American Negro Problem, the obligation of treating the Negro justly and charitably has been stressed. But the practice of those virtuous acts is rendered extremely difficult because of the white American's strong prejudice against the Negro. To that fact consideration must now be given. Putnam Weale has pertinently written, "The individual who refuses to see things as they still appear to the mass of his countrymen and who simply argues academically on all so-called colored questions without considering those vital prejudices is not worthy of being read."[18]

Race Prejudice

Prejudice is a natural phenomenon in the sense that it is wide-spread. Throughout the world prejudice appears in a variety of forms, such as caste prejudice, in a variety of patterns, and in varying degrees of intensity. The white American's prejudice against the Negro is but one form of a world-wide phenomenon. It differs from many other forms in that in addition to prepossessions and opinions formed without sufficient knowledge it includes an excessive amount of feeling. For that reason the prejudice is extremely difficult to define. Furthermore, since in America it is woven from many skeins and warps, and since all the threads are not woven about every situation, unified treatment is almost impossible. The examination of the more important constituent elements may be helpful.

---

18 Weale, "The Conflict of Color," p. 226.

Its basic warp, some writers hold, is a physical reaction of aversion to the Negro, and is founded upon a trait which has its roots deep in the nature of man. Most men, they maintain, experience unpleasantness when they are brought into close contact with men who differ considerably from themselves either in appearance or habit. It was inevitable then, they conclude, that the white colonists should have experienced at first a repulsion toward the Negro. The Negroes differed diametrically from them in color, in facial features, in bodily odor, in language, and in culture.[19]

Yet reactions of that type are extremely subtle; and although individuals may regard them as natural or instinctive they are frequently conditioned reactions and are attributable to preconceptions or early experiences. It is very improbable that the white man's prejudice against the Negro is basically instinctive and few competent psychologists would regard it as such. Their attitude is conservatively presented in the following reports of a committee appointed by the Federal Council of Churches to investigate the problem: "The majority of the members of this committee believe that racial prejudice is socially conditioned, that there is no such thing as innate racial prejudice, but that it comes about in children through the absorption of attitudes expressed by the community expecially by parents and adults close to one child and through him passed on to the other children."[20]

However, even if the prejudice were basically instinctive it would not for that reason have a peculiar moral significance. Evidently it has no greater strength than the aversion people sometimes feel for certain foods and it is easily overcome by a desire to adjust oneself

---

19 Reuter, "The American Race Problem," p. 144.
Cf. Pinkerton, "Interesting Voyages," vol. 16, p. 309 (London, 1814).

20 *Religious Education,* June, 1926, p. 281.
Cf. Bogardus, "Fundamentals of Social Psychology," p. 321.
Young, "What is Race Prejudice?" *Journal of Applied Sociology,* vol. 10, p. 134.
Duffus, "Where do We Get Our Prejudices?" *Harper's Magazine,* vol. 153, p. 503.

to existing conditions, at least in regard to a few Negroes. Reuter admits that in the Colonial days "as the Negro became a regular part of the environment, conventional attitudes replaced the original reaction. The bodily odor, the divergent appearance ceased to be offensive or even noticed once they were no longer strange."[21] In the South, Negroes are employed as maids, as cooks, as chauffeurs, and in the country at large as porters and waiters without occasioning any serious physical inconvenience to whites.

An element, which plays if not the basic role at least a strong role in the formation of the American prejudice, is that psychological process by which organic reactions are extended to the social field and aroused by social stimuli. People of refinement have an abhorrence for dirt which is unknown in the savage and the peasant. Gossip about the moral offenses of a particular individual causes, occasionally, men to experience aversion when the man is met personally. Feelings of resentment and hatred are often aroused in the inhabitants of Protestant nations when they meet a Catholic for the first time. The existence of striking physical features accenuate that very human tendency since they have the effect of fixing and intensifying emotions originally excited by other causes. Hence a difference of color may become associated with emotions originally aroused by non-racial causes and may evoke those feelings when the original cause is no longer present.[22]

In the popular American concept the Negroes are ignorant, unclean, lazy, untruthful, and incapable of sexual restraint. Those traits are easily associated with the dark skin. Thus, an unpleasant reaction is occasioned by contact with a Negro regardless of his virtues. The obvious poverty, illiteracy, and weakness of many of the colored people of this generation heighten that feeling. But even that unpleasantness is easily controlled in regard to a few Negroes. Personal acquaintance and

21 Op. cit., p. 144.
22 Oldham, op. cit., p. 44.

knowledge of kindnesses on the part of a particular Negro acts as a powerful solvent. Many Southerners have intense affection for their domestics. But the unpleasantness increases rapidly with the number of Negroes especially if the contacts are intimate and lengthy.[23] That unpleasantness, however, can be completely overcome by those who dwell permanently among the colored group or by those who are motivated by high ideals. But the average individual who passes among the colored group only occasionally experiences considerable unpleasantness. It was in that sense that Jefferson and many other early Americans were said to have been prejudiced against the Negro.[24] That fact explains the recent change in the attitude of the people of Philadelphia. A colored woman of that city has written: "They had always enjoyed the same social and educational facilities as the whites and courteous treatment from them. But with the increase in population by a group of generally uneducated and untrained persons those privileges were withdrawn."[25] Some American Negroes on the other hand experience frequently less unpleasantness from this score because they have been taught to associate culture, intelligence, and wealth with a white skin. Yet many experience unpleasantness because they have associated the white skin with the reaction which an oppressed group feels toward a tyrant.

A third powerful element entering into the prejudice is that jealous aversion to any change or disturbance of the social order felt by the members of the group in the superior position. This trait is extremely important because it is wedded with customs which enjoy tremendous force. Allport writes: "Its edicts are habits formed in the individual from earliest childhood. Breaches of custom seem objectionable to us chiefly be-

---

23 Cf. "The Natural History of Race Prejudice," in "Ebony and Topaz," p. 89.

24 Phillips, "American Negro Slavery," p. 123.

25 Mossell, *The Annals of the Academy of Political and Social Sciences,* vol. 98, p. 177.

cause they do violence to long standing habits."[26] Social changes occasion, at times, as much unpleasantness in the lives of men as disturbances within their own physical organisms. If the change implies the advance of an easily distinguishable group to the position of equality the resentment is equivalent to the indignation or the sense of humiliation which comes from an attack upon one's pride or self-respect. The member of the superior group feels that he is being degraded. Such feelings are extremely difficult to control despite wide reading and travel because they are so deeply embedded in the habits of childhood.

In the instance of the prejudice against the Negro that tendency is magnified a hundred fold. The black skin was prior to the Civil War the symbol of the slave, and since then has been the symbol of the servant. Consequently, as Reuter remarks with some truth: "The powerful prejudice against the Negro is largely a development and character of freedom. In the South the important prejudice was against the Negro out of his traditional status. There was a fixed conception of the place of the Negro in the social order and a dislike for him in any other relation."[27]

In the North the objection to the Negro in any capacity except that of a servant has, also, contributed much to the prejudice. In Massachusetts in 1840, patrons threatened to leave the dining room of a Sound Steamer because a free Negro was being served as a guest.[28] During the Civil War the Union troops protested against the use of Negroes as soldiers in the Northern army.[29] During the Reconstruction period white workmen refused to labor beside members of the colored group. Even today white craftsmen object to the entrance of the Negroes into the trades in which they are employed. But in this last instance an economic

26 Allport, "Social Psychology," p. 394.
27 Reuter, op. cit., p. 148.
28 "The Negro Pew," p. 76.
29 Brawley, "A Social History of the American Negro," p. 252.

factor is introduced. The white man's exclusive dominion over the industrial and commercial life of the country is threatened.

The tremendous force of the caste prejudice becomes strikingly evident when conditions in the United States are compared with those prevailing in countries such as Brazil, Cuba, or Porto Rico, the population of which includes a large Negro element. Although some travelers protest against the alleged absence of prejudice in those countries they are unanimous in the judgment that the Negro is not denied entrance into any profession or trade because of his color. Bryce writes: "The distinction between the races in South America is a distinction of rank or class rather than that of color."[30] Johnston states: "They enter all careers, serve in all trades, professions, and employments in Brazil from the humblest to nearly the highest; from the scavenger to the priesthood, college professorships, and party leaderships."[31]

Another human trait which is woven into the American prejudice against the Negro is slavish respect for public opinion, submissiveness to convention. The average individual when forced to wear clothes out of style or contrary to the accepted modes suffers considerable shame and embarrassment. Likewise, many white individuals, if forced to work beside a Negro or to dwell beside him on a basis of equality or to have any contact with him contrary to the traditional one of master and servant, feel themselves humiliated. Often the native American who has conquered all other traditional reactions toward the Negro will surrender to convention. Since most people are followers and not leaders, the greatest burden imposable upon any member of the middle class of society is the necessity of acting contrary to the conventions of the dominant group. When the American people adopt a different style toward the Negro prejudice will shrink considerably.

---

30 Bryce, "South American Impressions," p. 470.
31 Johnston, "The Negro in the New World," p. 106.

These are but a few of the characteristic traits of men which are woven into the prejudice of the white American against the Negro. Numerous others could be identified and enumerated: the tendency to generalize about a group; the tendency to distrust an economic competitor: the tendency begotten of isolation and ignorance to depreciate the members of another group. Obviously, the same impulses and tendencies give rise to dislikes between the members of the same race. In the case of the Negro they are easily associated with his color and thus acquire greater force and spontaneity.

Yet one point which deserves emphasis is that since the prejudice is probably not instinctive there is a possibility that in some future time it may be eliminated. Professor Drachsler has observed: "If Pavlow's canine can learn to modify such a relatively rigid mechanical and invariable type of behavior as a reflex act, certainly a normal human child can be socially 'conditioned' in its attitude toward different social and racial types, for human attitudes are much more modifiable, much more pliable, much more adaptable, than crass reflexes. Theoretical psychology and education then hold out some hope of achieving race harmonization."[32]

A second point that must be stressed is that race prejudice, though not instinctive, will be corrected slowly and only after the expenditure of much effort. Goldenweiser, declares: "The element of prejudice is here so violent that it is useless to attack it directly."[33] "Idealists," writes Young, "have succeeded in numerous cases in developing highly tolerant attitudes, but not without serious struggle with their prejudices. It is probably too much to hope that the mass of men can be brought to such a state of mind."[34] Because, as Professor Faris writes: "Race prejudice being at the same time a collective and emotional condition is modified slowly. It changes slowly but it does change. A too sudden modi-

32 Proceedings of N. C. S. W., 1926, p. 102.
33 Proceedings of N. C. S. W., 1926, p. 474.
34 *Journal of Applied Sociology*, 1925, vol. 10, p. 140.

fication, either of attitude or institution, is not only impermanent in character but tends to be followed by a reaction which temporarily leaves the last state worse than the first."[35]

The Moral Implications of the Prejudice

The prejudice against the Negro and its consequent unpleasantness are to a considerable extent irrational and arbitrary. Nevertheless, being the progeny of long standing habits, they are for the present generation almost irradicable. They are realities for which serious allowance must be made in any moral judgment.

In the first place it must be recognized that the existence of such feelings of aversion does not necessarily imply the sin of anger or of uncharitableness. Father Noldin has declared: "Often what is designated as a sin is nothing except a natural antipathy or aversion of the soul springing from the diversity of nature; and such an antipathy in so far as it is involuntary is sinless."[36] Vermeersch makes a similar observation, distinguishing between antipathy and voluntary anger. Physical aversion, he acknowledges, may at times become so strong that it completely dominates a man; and consequently, objectively uncharitable acts such as the refusal to speak to a neighbor may be for a short time inculpable.[37] However, as Father Noldin insists: "Every person is bound in conscience to attempt to repress such antagonisms both because they are generally an inversion of the proper order and because they are easily accepted by the will and thus degenerate into acts of hatred."[38]

A more important implication of the unpleasantness felt by white persons is that it may constitute at times an exemption from acts which otherwise would be required by human or divine law. Theologians have al-

35 Op. cit., p. 93.
36 "Summa Theologiae Moralis," vol. II, p. 63.
37 "Theologia Moralis," vol. II, p. 63.
38 Op. cit., p. 117.

ways taught that a grave inconvenience or unpleasantness experienced in the observance of affirmative laws of minor moment excuses from compliance with the laws, for man is entitled to the opportunity of seeking a reasonable amount of happiness and contentment. If compliance with minor laws would deprive a man of happiness through a long period of time then the laws are regarded as suspended for the individual.[39] Father Tanquerey has declared: "Laws cannot command what is too arduous or difficult, since what is promulgated for the common good ought to be proportioned to the weaknesses of human nature."[40]

Theologians in their examination of the conditions in which restitution for an injustice must be made, teach that the consequent loss of social position excuses temporarily from the reparation of a financial injustice, provided that the creditor is not suffering a similar danger. This teaching of the theologians is intensively informative relative to our discussion. The object involved is not the loss of a quantity of food or clothing indispensable to human living, but the loss of conventional necessities, the deprivation of which causes a serious anguish and sadness because of long standing habits. Obviously these feelings of aversion which are associated with customs and habits are regarded by the theologians as a basis of that moral impotency which sometimes excuses from the fulfilment of laws.

However, it must be noted that discomfort or inconvenience does not constitute an exemption from every law. Such a condition cannot be pleaded as a justification for the violation of the divine negative laws which forbid intrinsically bad acts such as hatred of neighbor or adultery. Nor does such a factor exempt one from observing those positive laws the violation of which would lead to the common damage or to the contempt of religion. In respect to other laws the quantity of the inconvenience must be proportioned to the seriousness of

39 Lehmkuhl, "Theologia Moralis," p. 149.
40 Tanquerey, "Synopsis Theologiae Moralis," t. 11, p. 158.

the law. If the welfare or the interests of others are involved the inconvenience should be exceedingly great. The amount, however, as Bouquillon observed, "cannot be defined by any general rule. It depends on the moment of the laws, the quality of the person, and the circumstances."[41]

To some persons this principle may appear casuistical, especially those whose ideals are of the Gospel but whose practices are otherwise. But the principle has been defended by all Christian teachers, and it is indispensable to a practical system of ethics. The statement of it here is intended to emphasize the fact that not all of the actions of white Christians which have been construed as uncharitable by Negroes, are at variance with the Christian moral code.

A keener appreciation of the extent and limitation of this principle may be gathered from the examination of another fundamental proposition which has a tremendous bearing on all racial matters; namely, in any apparent conflict of duties, of interests, or of rights the superior obligation is to be preferred to the inferior. Since men have a variety of obligations, such as their obligations to God, to self, and to neighbor, and since their interests are frequently crossing, their obligations seem, at times, to conflict. The moral order appears to be threatened with chaos. But in reality the conflict can only be apparent for the ultimate source of all rights and obligations is the will of God. And God being supremely wise would not impose contradictory obligations or concede contradictory rights. Only one obligation really exists. The others are suspended for their fulfilment is impossible. Obviously the obligation which survives is the superior.[42] Cronin writes: "We must conceive the moral laws from which rights spring as making up one organic system, just as the parts of the body make up one organic bodily system. And just as

---

41 Op. cit., p. 352.

42 Cathrein, "Philosophia Moralis," n. 258. Cf. Noldin, op. cit., vol. I, p. 202.

the functions of one part of an organism limit the functions of others, and no part is exercised prejudicially to the other, so due regard for others must be had in exercising any rights."[43]

The racial situation in the United States furnishes an extensive field for the application of this last principle. All men, both black and white, have a vague claim to these conditions of life which guarantee confort and contentment. Their claim includes many potential rights. But, in the pursuit of those conditions and rights, the interests of both black and white often conflict. Because of the discomfort consequential to racial prejudice, some white men find fullness of happiness only when they are separated from the Negroes. The Negroes on the other hand, because the white man controls the organic resources of the country, the education, the industry, the commerce, and the recreation of the nation, can find a reasonable development of self, only in contact with the members of the Caucasian race. This conflict in varying degrees runs down the gamut of American life.

In many instances, the application of the principle is almost obvious. The claims of the Negro are clearly superior. For example, if the discomfort of a few whites actually conflicts with a Negro's right to work, the colored man's claim is superior. In other matters, though, especially those in which merely the claims of both groups to immunities from offensive situations are involved, a decision is more difficult. Yet, in balancing the claims of both races, much more importance must be given to the discomfort suffered by the Negro than people formerly allowed.

In some contacts, the conflicting interests appear equal. Then, some equitable compromise seems inevitable. For the peace and comfort of both groups the most satisfactory form of compromise is separation. Such separation may not be idealistic. But, because of the weaknesses of human nature, because of the varieties of tem-

---

43 Cronin, "The Science of Ethics," vol. 1, p. 625.

peraments, and because of the tendency of all to anger, such an arrangement appears necessary for a minimum of peaceful and right living. Reason dictates that such a practice is morally justifiable. The Scriptures, also, furnish data which analogously indicate the moral validity of racial separation. In the Book of Genesis, it is recorded that Abraham and Lot, because of strife between their respective herdsmen, agreed to separate.

The Negroes are prone, at times, to scoff at the members of the white race who profess the ideals of Christianity but who remain the slaves of racial antagonisms. Undoubtedly, between perfect submission to the counsels of Christ and the existence of such antagonisms, great contradiction exists. But the frailty of human nature should not be forgotten. Only a small proportion of each generation rose to the counsels of Christ. The masses were forced to struggle arduously to remain loyal to the commandments. Indeed, the weaknesses with which the white race are struggling can be better appreciated by the Negro if he will remember the existence of a color line within his own race. Walter White, a Negro, has written: "Living in an atmosphere where swarthiness of skin almost automatically brings denial of opportunity, it is inevitable as it is regrettable that there should grow up among the Negroes themselves distinctions based on skin color and hair texture. There are certain cities where only mulattoes attend certain churches, while those whose skin is dark brown or black attend others."[44] Such a condition does not justify the prejudice of the whites, but it does indicate the weakness of human nature and the seriousness of the struggle with which the white Christian is confronted.

---

44 Cf. Locke's "The New Negro," p. 366.

CHAPTER IV

GROSS WRONGS

Against the Negro there has been perpetrated a long series of wrongs, ranging from petty insult to the destruction of human life. Some are most flagrant and vital. These will be examined briefly in this chapter. For convenience they will be grouped in three sections; injustices against life, injustices against liberty, and injustices against welfare.

Against Life

Between the years 1889 and 1926, approximately 2880 Negroes were lynched. An overwhelming majority of those lynchings were perpetrated in the South. However, it must be admitted to the credit of the South that the practice of an unofficial group of citizens summarily executing an alleged criminal originated not in the South but in the East during the Revolutionary period. In subsequent generations the practice drifted westward and because of the imperfect legal machinery rapidly developed into an institution. During the Reconstruction period that Western practice was adopted by the South as a means of intimidating the Negroes. There it flourished for decades. In recent years, however, the practice, because of a counter-crusade, has declined sharply. During the year 1926, thirty Negroes were lynched, whereas in 1900 one hundred and seven Negroes met their death in that fashion.[1] Although the actual number of lynchings may seem insignificant, their social consequences are tremendous. The most potent indication is the reaction manifested by many white persons in conversation when the news of the lynching of a Negro has been published.

---

1 "The Negro Year Book," p. 399.

Evidently, numerous whites both in the North and in the South are not conscious of the immorality of the practice. Nor are their attitudes purely academic, since yearly a large number of lynchings are attempted and are frustrated only by the zealous efforts of the police. Relative to the effect of the practice upon the Negro, Woofter has observed: "Lynching is the most spectacular and intensified injustice to the Negro. It is the one which agitates both the leader and the masses most profoundly."[2]

Despite the opinion current among many white Americans, there can be for the Christian no question about the immorality of the practice. When a man has committed a serious crime his right to life is not forfeited. His right is still sacred against everyone except the State. A criminal may be executed by the State alone, and by the State only when he has been proven guilty of a very serious crime, in a fair trial.[3] Truly, a few theologians have taught that a group of citizens might be permitted to put a criminal to death if the public authorities made no serious effort to prosecute the guilty, or if the regular procedure of the court was so slow that the deterrent effect of the punishment was lost.[4] Yet even those conditions are not verified in the South. Relative to the enforcement of the law a Southerner has observed: "Mobs have not acted because the courts failed to act. Cases are on record where Negroes have been convicted immediately on apprehension and before the law could take its course the criminal has been lynched. There can be no doubt in the mind of any sane man that a Negro who has actually attacked a white woman would have no chance to escape punishment in a Southern court."[5]

Many white people believe that all the Negroes lynched have been proven guilty of attacking white women. Their

---

2 Woofter, "The Basis of Racial Adjustment," p. 136.
3 Gury, "Compendium Theologiae Moralis," vol. I, no. 404.
4 Ross, "Christian Ethics," p. 409.
5 Weatherford, "The Negro from Africa to America," p. 362.

belief is false. Actually the murder and the injury of white men are the principal crimes because of which Negroes are lynched. Less than one-third of the Negroes lynched were accused of raping white women. These whites who surrender to the belief that all colored men have an instinctive tendency to attack the women of other races might reflect with profit upon the following observation of an Englishman who for years held high office in the British colonies in Africa and the West Indies: "In the British possessions assaults by black or colored men on white women or children are practically unknown. No apprehension of them whatever troubles society. I say this as an administrator familiar with the juridical statistics, as a resident familiar with all parts of Jamaica."[6]

Another false belief is that lynchings deter the Negroes from committing crimes. Serious students of the race problem, such as Woofter, Weatherford, and Dowd, concur in condemning that belief. Rather mob rule increases crime. Such spectacles as lynchings give a wide publicity to the crime and tend to incite others to similar behavior. Such spectacles prompt the Negroes to attempt reprisals and also brutalize the white race.

Since the State alone may execute a criminal, the lynching of a Negro is the injust taking of human life. It constitutes that injustice which is more commonly designated as homicide or murder. All who actively co-operate in the lynching are in some degree guilty of the same sin. Among that group of co-operators must be included not only the man who fires the shot or who holds the rope, but all who deliberately assist the action in any way; those who by their presence encourage others to action; the sheriff who without great inconvenience could protect the Negro prisoner; and especially the agitators who arouse the crowd.[7] Truly, in many communities, men participate in lynchings without any consciousness of sin and are not regarded as murderers. Yet they di-

6 Olivier, "White Capital and Coloured Labour," p. 49.
7 Lehmkuhl, op. cit., p. 127.

rectly and unjustly destroy human life, so no other statement is possible. Their false judgment about the character of lynching is due to defective religious teaching. Professor Dowd has written: "While I have heard denunciations of nearly every sin to which human nature is susceptible, I have never heard from the pulpit one utterance against lynching. To judge Southern clergymen by the themes of their sermons one would suppose that they did not regard lynching as comparable to the sin of dancing, playing cards, or going to the theatre."[8]

The first remedy must be the reiteration of definite religious teaching about the true character of lynching. The second must be the enactment by various state legislatures of those measures which have successfully stamped out the evil in other states. Such measures include provisions for the rotation of judges and of prosecuting officials, for the organization of a state constabulary, and especially for increasing the responsibility of the sheriff. The last method has proved most effective.[9] The executive officials and the members of the various state legislatures who refuse to join in a movement for the passage of such legislation sin grieviously since they violate one of their most fundamental duties.

White people in the North often sit smugly in their armchairs and condemn the South for those gross violations of the Negro's right to life. They forget that the lives of many Negroes in the North have been snuffed out by another form of homicide, race rioting. In the Chicago riot of July, 1919, at least sixteen colored people were slain. In the East St. Louis riot of 1917, thirty-nine Negroes were killed by the populace. The record of the State of Illinois may be exceptional, yet serious riots have occurred in other States. The observations made about the moral character of the actions of those men who co-operate in lynchings are applicable equally to the participants in race riots. They are murderers. In the

---

8 Dowd, "The Negro in American Life," p. 127.
9 Weatherford, op. cit., p. 365.

North, also, religious teaching on such matters has been defective.

Against Liberty

During the slave period the punishment of all but the most serious crimes committed by Negroes was entrusted to the white masters. Since the slave represented a financial investment of the white man, few Negroes were unjustly arrested or detained by the public officials. Their sudden and arbitrary emancipation, however, upset that arrangement. No intelligent provision was made for another criminal code which would have been accommodated to the changed conditions. By the law they were declared to be equal to the white man, and consequently they were subjected to the same juridical procedure. Actually, because of the lack of training and because of an unfavorable environment, they differed decidedly from the Caucasian. Inevitably, a greater propensity to crime developed among them and the existing system was found to be inadequate for their regulation and their correction.

Various adjustments were attempted in the South. Pilfering and other petty offenses were completely ignored. But for serious crimes more drastic punishment was apportioned than that which was accorded to the whites. In the North, all violations of the law by the Negroes were harshly dealt with, and no attempt was made to correct the social conditions which bred the crimes. Despite such blunderings, however, the Negro's power of self-control and his adjustment to the white standards developed rapidly. Yet today many public officials are still imbued with the conviction that the Negro should be treated differently. And in the arbitrary effort of officials to enforce that conviction, the Negro's liberty has frequently been restricted.

If Chicago may be regarded as a fairly typical city of the North it seems evident that many Northern Negroes are unjustly arrested. Before the Racial Commission of that city testimony was given by several judges that Negroes were often arrested because of suspicion or because of prejudice against their color. "Negroes have fewer resources and less influence with which to insure their fair treatment."[10]

In the South, Dr. Woofter states: "No adequate figures as to arrests are available but if they could be secured, the number of useless arrests of Negroes would prove astonishing. The fee system which allows officials a fee for each arrest and allows judges, solicitors and sheriffs a proportion of the court costs of trials is a vicious factor in this useless arrest."[11]

The pigment of the Negro's skin, besides influencing the police officer, also affects the court. The Chicago Commission quoted above declared: "Colored people are more easily convicted on serious charges and they are given longer sentences."[12] While stating that some judges treated the Negro considerately, "conditions in other courts," the Report continued, "were quite different. One judge frequently assumed an attitude of facetiousness while hearing Negro cases. In one instance the judge was shaking dice during the hearing of the case."[13]

In the courts of the Southland, "statistics indicate a definite tendency on the part of Southern courts to impose heavier sentences on the Negro than upon white men and heavier sentences than those imposed upon them by Northern courts."[14] However, it should be noted that it is only the friendless Negro who is treated unfairly in the Southern courts. The colored person who has a white friend or an indulgent employer, receives justice and sometimes more than justice. An inkling of the treatment accorded to the friendless Negro may be gathered from the account of a day's proceedings in a Southern court given by Mrs. Hammond. Two cases were called. In the first a white man was accused and convicted of abducting a girl for immoral purposes and was sentenced

---

10 "The Negro in Chicago," p. 335.
11 Op. cit., p. 130.
12 Op. cit., p. 64[illegible].
13 Idem, p. 333.
14 Op. cit., p. 130.

to jail for one year. In the second case a Negro boy was accused and convicted of stealing $11.46 and was sent to jail for three years. And in the latter case, the judge stated that he was making a special allowance because of the culprit's age.[15]

About the brutal and inhuman treatment accorded the Negroes in the prison camp after conviction much has been written. However that phase of the abuse of public power by public officials is scarcely racial. White prisoners are treated with almost equal barbarity.[16] Indeed, that fact confirms the contention that the race which insists upon treating another race as a brute soon descends to the same level. The inhuman treatment of the Negro by the white Southerner has recoiled upon the white prisoner just as the barbarities practiced by the English in their perfection of the African Slave Trade recoiled upon the factory hands in England.[17]

No words of condemnation are too severe for the police both of the North and the South who persist in arresting Negroes merely on suspicion or prejudice. They commit a most serious offense by using their office and power to abuse the weak and friendless group. Sometimes an attempt is made to palliate their guilt by the allegation that the Negro has a predisposition to crime. That contention was examined in an earlier chapter. Here it is sufficient to state again that, while defective individuals may be more numerous among them because of the absence of asylums, there is no reason to believe that the Negro is peculiarly disposed to criminal behavior. Criminally inclined individuals constitute a small section of the colored race, despite the popular conception of the criminal Negro as the typical Negro.

For the correction of those gross restrictions of the Negro's liberty there is one measure which should be promptly adopted, that is the appointment of a number of responsible Negroes to the police force. Presumably

---

15 Hammond, "In Black and White," p. 46.
16 Cf. Tannenbaum, "Darker Phases of the South."
17 Cf. Hammond and Hammond, "The Rise of Modern Industry."

they would treat their own more fairly and would be able to secure more genuine respect and reverence for the law from the colored group. Already a few colored probation officials are employed in the South and their service, Woofter states, "has been invaluable to the community."[18]

Against Their Welfare

Only a small proportion of the members of the colored group are lynched or unjustly arrested. The average Negro suffers from those wrongs only in the sense that he is made fearful lest at some moment a frenzied white mob while intoxicated with racial hatred might attack him. There is, however, another gross injustice which affects the average Negro directly and seriously; namely, the practice of apportioning relatively small shares of the public funds for the education of the Negroes, for the policing, the improvement and the sanitation of their districts.

To the common people of this age, education is the manna of life. The individual who has been deprived of an elementary education suffers a worse handicap than the man whose clothing is limited to one threadbare and ragged suit. Such is the realization of the value attached to education by the people of this age that the normally lethargic conscience of the public would be indignantly aroused if the door of the public school was closed upon the child of poor parents. Such a condition would be regarded by every citizen as a gross injustice. Indeed, it is almost inconceivable that any American community would refuse to any white child an opportunity for an elementary education.

Unfortunately, the American public conscience does not realize as keenly the Negro's need of education. Consequently, a public policy has been adopted toward the Negro which closes, at least partially, the door of the public school upon the child of colored parents. The

---

18 Op. cit., p. 134.

various State governments expend much less for the education of the colored child than they do for the white child. In 1922, the per capita expenditure for the education of each white child in the South was $29.72 and the per capita expenditure for the education of each colored child was only $7.12.[19] The seriousness of the discrepancy becomes more evident if the relative amounts invested in school property by States having large colored populations are noted. For example, for every six dollars expended for the colored child by the State of Mississippi, thirty-two dollars are spent upon the white child. In Georgia, for every seven dollars spent on the colored, forty-eight dollars are spent on the white.[20] In some of those sections not a single school is owned by the public authorities for the use of the colored children, and they are forced to use an abandoned cabin or church. In the very districts in which those conditions prevail very expensive schools are usually maintained for the white children. However, while such an inequitable distribution of the school funds prevails in many Southern communities, it does not characterize every section. There are sections of the States of Virginia and North Carolina where an earnest effort is made to offer the Negro adequate facilities.

But for genuine education, a competent and trained teacher is of greater importance than modern buildings and equipment. Unfortunately, in that matter, also, the Negroes have been treated unfairly. Their teachers are poorly paid and incompetent. Weatherford records that in Arkansas the salaries for teachers of the first grade for the year 1919 averaged $90 for whites and $55 for the colored. Such figures, he states, are typical.[21] It happens, therefore, that hundreds of Negro schools are taught by young girls whose training has been limited to that given in the local school. Reuter maintains that "about seventy per cent of the teachers in the black belt

---

19 Woofter, op. cit., p. 177.
20 "The Negro Year Book," p. 294 and p. 435.
21 Weatherford, op. cit., p. 376.

have less than a sixth-grade education."[22] Furthermore, until recent years, "the Negro school has been almost wholly without supervision. Many superintendents did not visit Negro schools at all and gave no attention to training Negro teachers."[23] Verily it might have been said of the Negro schools that "the blind were leading the blind."

In the matter of high schools, fair opportunities are now offered in some of the larger cities but in the country there are fully two million colored children who are limited to a meager elementary training. The State universities of the South which are supported by public funds are, of course, closed to the Negro, and the few normal, agricultural and mechanical schools which are conducted for them receive only a thirty-fifth of the entire appropriation. Possibly, with the exception of the elementary schools, no discrimination in educational funds is as tragic as that in the agricultural and vocational schools. It is tragic, both because such training is indispensable to the colored masses in the South and also because a considerable proportion of the funds supporting the white vocational schools is federal money, received as a consequence of the Smith-Hughes Vocational Educational Act of 1917.[24]

It may be profitable to note that in the South the Negro is actually receiving more education than these statements would indicate. But the resources for that work come not from the public funds but from private donations. The great institutions of Hampton and Tuskegee, with a combined enrollment of 3,600 and an income of over half a million, are financed largely by private endowments. The colored rural schools are benefited by assistance received from the John Slater Fund which aims to improve county training schools, from the Anna T. Jeans Foundation which partially supports supervising teachers, and from the General Educational Board.

---

22 Reuter, op. cit., p. 274.
23 Weatherford, idem, p. 376.
24 "The Negro Year Book," p. 321.

Approximately two and one quarter millions are spent by religious bodies upon denominational academies. But probably of all the private contributions for the education of the Negro, the most noteworthy is the Julius Rosenwald Fund. Its fame rests not on the amounts contributed, but upon its efficient administration and its insistence upon the co-operation of the colored people and the public authorities. So far it is probably the best adjustment to a trying situation. For the year ending on June 30, 1926, money was contributed toward the erection of 493 buildings. But of the total expenditure involved the Fund contributed only sixteen per cent. The Negroes gave eighteen per cent, the whites four per cent, and the public authorities sixty per cent.[25]

In the maintenance of other public institutions, as hospitals, libraries, asylums, orphanages, and parks, the same ratio undoubtedly prevails, although accurate data relative to those institutions are not available. Truly, in the South the number of such institutions supported even for the whites by public funds is small. In the Northern border communities, where the public revenue permits much more extensive service, the Negroes receive much less than their share. For example, in Baltimore, the city of hospitals, there are available 4,630 beds in the hospitals for public use. Of that number, because of their proportion to the population, there should be available for the Negroes at least 660. Actually, in 1926, there were only 248 beds which their sick could use.[26]

Of much greater moment is the failure of the public authorities both in the North and the South to give to the colored districts any service equivalent to the service rendered to the whites in the matter of paving, lighting, the enforcement of sanitary conditions, and the suppression of disorderly houses.

Since the Industrial Revolution, large numbers of people have been drawn to the cities, and there many of them have been forced to dwell in extremely congested dis-

---

25 *Opportunity,* October, 1926, p. 321.
26 *Opportunity,* October, 1926, p. 303.

tricts, in structures which were small, drab, and unsanitary. Civilized man has always struggled to create an attractive and cheerful domestic environment. So those people, also, endeavored to make their dwellings as wholesome and as beautiful as possible. But their efforts were frustrated and dampened by social forces which passed beyond the control of the average citizen. Eventually, they grew discouraged, surrendered to carelessness, and became easy prey to great immoral passions. For a certain degree of cheerfulness and comfort is almost indispensable for moral living. A Catholic writer has recently insisted upon the following conditions as essential to the average family for Christian living: A cheerful, self-contained house for each family with at least three bedrooms in addition to a living-room, adequate sanitary conveniences, a general level of cleanliness, and good repair inside and out.[27]

Ultimately the health and the morality of the masses became so dangerously undermined that the various municipal governments were compelled to recognize the necessity of intervention. The officials slowly grew convinced that the inhabitants must be protected from those insidious social forces by official action: by statutes which would determine the size of dwellings; by statutes which would require the owners to keep the property clean, sanitary and repaired; by statutes which would impower the police to suppress immoral resorts; by the creation of departments which would pave and clean the streets. Today the engagement of American municipal governments in such activities is regarded as normal and as essential for the physical and moral well-being of the white inhabitants.

But if such action is desirable for the white people, it is absolutely indispensable for the colored people in the United States. Their tastes for attractive and clean homes have not as yet been fully developed. Their family life, which could be encouraged by attractive homes,

---

27 Toke, "The Housing Problem," p. 32.

is in a precarious position. To that fact much of their alleged tendency to crime is traceable. The homes and the residential environment are the great potters which mould character.

Unfortunately, most communities have crudely neglected the Negro districts. The Racial Commission of Chicago, which acquired a reputation for unbiased statements, reported that in the matter of enforcing sanitary regulations, the up-keep of streets, and the collection of garbage, the "Negro districts in Chicago were shamefully neglected." The Committee also recommended that the police, the State's attorney, and other authorities promptly rid the Negro residential areas of vice resorts, "whose exceptional prevalence in such areas is due to official laxity."[28] In Buffalo it was found that seventy-five per cent of the colored families occupied a section which contained the poorest houses, and that many of those houses had formerly been condemned as uninhabitable. The Philadelphia Housing Association declared that, "only ten per cent of the houses occupied by Negro families in that city were equipped for sanitation, convenience and comfort."[29]

In the colored districts of Southern cities, "there is seldom any effort made," writes a white Southerner, "to enforce housing codes prescribing the size of the dwelling, the space between the houses, and sanitary arrangements. Sanitary inspectors avoid those districts and the failure of the city to extend sewer lines into them often makes compliance with sanitary regulations an impossibility. The streets in those sections are usually unpaved and wholly lacking in garbage removal facilities."[30] Those generalizations have been amply verified in many detailed studies such as that made in Lynchburg, Virginia, by Benjamin Childs.[31]

---

28 "The Negro in Chicago," p. 642.
29 Dowd, "The Negro in American Life," p. 24.
30 Woofter, op. cit., p. 70.
31 "The Negro in Lynchburg, Virginia."

Ethical Implications.

Many Americans have attempted to justify the practice of distributing a small proportion of the public funds to the colored group on the ground that the Negroes pay less taxes. The fact that their contributions in the form of direct taxes are decidedly smaller both quantitatively and proportionately cannot be gainsaid. Of the real and personal property which is taxed they own a very meager share. In North Carolina, they have title to only four per cent of the property taxed, and in Mississippi they have title to only eight per cent. Nevertheless, the colored group contributes more to the public fund than the average citizen realizes. The property which is on the statute books in the name of colored owners is not a complete gauge of the tax borne by the race. Because for every dollar's worth of land owned, approximately three dollars' worth is rented by colored farmers. And it is a well-established economic fact that on city rental property, although the landlord actually hands over the tax money to the collector his ability to pay rests on the payment of the rent by the tenant. Likewise, the taxes on corporate property and the license tax are paid by the patrons of the businesses, and the colored people bear their proportionate share. A fair method of arriving at the proportion of the total tax borne by colored people would be to add to the value of real property owned, the value of homes rented and the personal property and to find what proportion this sum is of the total property.

But even though the Negro does not pay proportionately as much taxes as the white man, his claim to public benefits is not thereby directly affected. The basis for the imposition of taxes differs completely from that for the distribution of public funds. To achieve its purpose the State needs financial resources, and those are secured through the imposition of taxes. The principle by which the State must determine the assessment of each individual is his ability to pay.[32] For the individual is

---

32 Tanquerey, "Synopsis Theologiae Moralis," t. III, p. 251.

bound by legal justice to render to society in proportion to his powers whatever is necessary for the common good, whatever is necessary for the creation of a condition in which the rights of all will be protected.[33]

However, the State, in distributing the funds collected by taxes, is under no obligation to give to each citizen benefits in proportion to the taxes paid by the citizen. Rather the State, in distributing those funds, has an obligation to strive to create a condition in which the rights of all will be protected and a condition in which all will have equal opportunity to secure those goods which are unobtainable by personal effort. If all the subjects of a nation have approximately the same needs identical services should be offered to all. Each citizen has a right in distributive justice against the State for such service. But if within the State one group, because of poverty or weakness, have special needs, the State is bound in as far as the welfare of all will permit to give to them special facilities.[34] Such is the official teaching of the Catholic Church as expounded by Pope Leo XIII in his encyclical letter, "Rerum Novarum." "When there is a question of protecting the rights of individuals," wrote the pontiff, "the poor and helpless have a claim to special consideration. The richer population have many ways of protecting themselves. Those who are poorly off have no resources of their own to fall back upon and must chiefly rely upon the assistance of the State." Such is, also, the practice of the American people at least to the extent of giving equal facilities to all white citizens. Every state has a school fund which is distributed to the various counties, both rich and poor, not on the basis of what they contribute to the state treasury but on the basis of the school attendance.

Consequently, the Negroes have a claim in distributive justice against the various State governments and against the various municipal organizations for facilities

---

33 Vermeersch, "Questiones de Justitia," p. 58.
34 Cathrein, "Philosophia Moralis," p. 516. Vermeersch, "Theologia Moralis," p. 287.

at least equal to those given to the whites. The public officials who fail to make any effort to distribute the funds in an equitable manner commit a serious injustice. The citizens who, by incendiary speeches or other means, prevent the officials from giving just proportions to the colored group sin seriously, also, because they cooperate in an unjust act. Indeed, the Negroes' claim in justice to some of the public benefits is greater than that of the white group because they may be designated as the poor and helpless class in the United States.

To these statements the objection might be made that in view of the limited resources of the Southern States, the welfare of all would be best promoted by continuing the present distribution. The objection, if properly qualified, has some merit of truth. It is probable that the welfare of both races would be best promoted at the present time by some slight discrimination made in favor of the white, both that the high standard of social culture achieved by the whites might not be lost while the colored group are developing, and that an efficient leadership for the entire group might be guaranteed. For several generations to come, the important political offices in the Southern States will most probably be held exclusively by white men because of prejudice. Consequently, it is to the interests of all, both black and white, that the white men who are to hold those offices should receive special training. However, every white man will not become an office-holder and so the State is not justified in offering elaborate high school facilities to all white children while the Negroes receive only a partial elementary training. Nor is the State justified in erecting an expensive medical school for white students when no provision is made for the qualified colored aspirant. Indeed, while the principle of the objection is valid it is difficult to perceive any concrete circumstances in which the various States are justified in making a slight discrimination. If such circumstances exist they should not be presumed but clearly proved because of the innumerable abuses.

The presence of such a large group of backward people constitutes, undoubtedly, a burden upon many districts in the South. Yet it should not be forgotten that some of the backwardness of those people is due directly to the policies of the whites. They have resented the attempts of the Federal government to assist in the education of the Negro. They have fought Congressional appropriations for colored institutions, such as Howard University. The Federal government is at present rendering all the assistance which the South is willing to accept.

The members of the white race should not forget that they will gain by any effort to give to the Negro his share of public benefits. To make the Negro's home more sanitary is to safeguard the home of the white man. The germ knows no color line. To give the Negro a better education is to improve the entire nation. Weatherford writes: "Real training never has injured anyone or made any man less valuable to society. To do less than this would delay the progress of the whole South, for no country is any stronger than its weakest citizen. In giving such training as this we not only will enrich the life of the Negro but we will, also, enrich our own life."[35]

The success achieved by local branches of the Interracial Commission within the past years in securing for the Negro an increased participation in the public favors and benefits indicates a most promising field of remedial activity for the future. Another effective remedy for a section of the country which professes Christianity so earnestly would be a crusade from the pulpit; a crusade which would aim to convince the public officials and populace that by depriving the Negro of his share of public benefits they commit a serious sin. The actions of the officials are possible because they reflect the attitude of the community.

---

[35] Op. cit., p. 389.

CHAPTER V.

INTERMARRIAGE AND SOCIAL SEPARATION

Through practically three centuries the Negroes and whites have occupied that section of the continent of North America known as the United States. During that time, as the large mulatto element in the colored group implies, there has been considerable sexual intercourse between the races. The exact extent is difficult to estimate. Dr. Herskovits, in a tentative summary of his elaborate studies of the Negro's ancestry, estimates that only twenty per cent of the American Negro group are pure-blooded Negroes. However, in the remaining eighty per cent he recognizes the presence of a considerable amount of Indian blood. His estimate is an interesting indication of the wide diffusion of white blood in our colored group.[1]

When the Negro servants were first introduced into the English colonies, a few of the indentured white servants attempted to mate with them. But the rulers of the colonies immediately protested. From the earliest times, marriages between blacks and whites in those colonies were forbidden both by formal enactment and by public sentiment. Clandestine unions, however, were not so easily controlled. As the institution of slavery developed and the Negro's position of submission to the white man became more pronounced it became extremely easy for the blacks and whites to co-habit without attracting public notice. Consequently, an overwhelming per cent of the inter-racial unions formed during the slave period were temporary illicit unions of white men with colored female slaves. Even after emancipation that condition continued for several decades, since the colored woman remained practically a slave even though she was free

---

1 *Opportunity,* Oct., 1926, p. 306.

before the law; the responsibility for race mixture during all of that period rests without doubt upon the white race. During the last twenty years, however, these illicit unions have diminished to a negligible quantity. Hence, since formal marriages also have continued to remain rare and to meet with social disapproval, sexual unions between blacks and whites are in this generation very unusual; and few mulatto children are born now of black and white parents.

Nevertheless, the question is recurrently asked by students of social problems: "Should the colored and white races in America intermarry?" Actually the answer to that query will not directly and immediately affect the life of the average member of either race. The majority in each racial group have no desire to espouse persons from the other group. However, since in the popular mind miscegenation looms as the most important aspect of the American race problem and since indirectly an answer will have practical application relative to social contacts, some discussion of the morality of inter-racial marriage and of its more practical antecedent, racial association, must be undertaken. Therefore, in the following paragraphs, an attempt will be made to answer two questions. Is it right for the races to intermarry? Is it right for the races to intermingle on such conditions that friendships conducive to intermarriage will inevitably be formed?

I. Miscegenation

The more common answer given to the first of these questions has been in the negative and a variety of arguments have been advanced to sustain the position. Our treatment of the question will be moulded about an examination of these arguments. In the interest of clearness they will be grouped roughly under three heads, biological, social, and moral.

Biological and Social Objections

Many false impressions prevail even in the minds of educated persons about the biological effects of marriages between Negroes and whites. This condition is due in a large measure to the pseudo-eugenists and race purists who, in books and articles composed for popular consumption, assert with the absoluteness of a newsboy that the crossing of races must result in an inferior offspring. The ridiculous exaggeration in their statements becomes apparent when the statements are compared with the facts of history. For it cannot be gainsaid that there are no pure races in Europe and few of any consequence in the world.[2] All the great historical groups which are regarded as the builders of our western civilization are, in a sense, mongrel, hybrid races. They are the products of a process of racial crossing and recrossing—a process which has been going on for ages. Consequently, unless subscription is made to the pessimistic doctrine that all existing peoples are extremely inferior, the race purists must be regarded as indulging in gross exaggerations when they state that the offspring of a racial cross is necessarily inferior.

Actually, many biologists regard a certain amount of race crossing as desirable. In nearly every racial group there exist native weaknesses. If such a group inbreeds, these defects can easily be accentuated, but in racial crossings these defects may be inhibited or covered by more dominant factors. Furthermore, greater variability and the possibility of great potentialities are secured as a consequence of racial crossing. Likewise, it seems to be an accepted principle among biologists that the hybrid generation is frequently endowed with greater vigor.

Certain forms of race crossing, however, are opposed by some biologists. By such students it is held that, while some forms of race crossing may be beneficial, the crossing of two highly divergent stocks usually produces an inferior offspring. The causes of the inferiority are

---

[2] Hankins, "The Racial Basis of Civilization," p. 271.

the resultant physical and mental disharmonies and the excessive variability. Such a thesis has been advanced by East and Jones in their work "Inbreeding and Outbreeding" and by Carr-Saunders in "The Population Problem." The exponents of this biological theory would, of course, object to the mating of Negroes and whites.

On the other hand, there are biologists who maintain that the alleged unfortunate results of the crossings of two highly divergent stocks have yet to be proved. Such a contention has been advanced by Professor L. S. Dunn of Storr's Agricultural Station.[3] Professor Hankins after an extensive examination of the alleged presence of physical disharmonies and of criminal tendencies in such types of hybrids also holds that the case is unproved. "Race crossing," he writes, "may and doubtless does lead to some alterations in bodily proportions and mental possibilities. But that it leads to disharmonies or instability is far from established and in view of the influence of the internal secretions on embryological development it seems highly improbable that from race crossings alone serious disharmonies could result."[4] The same writer even suggests that with the increase of knowledge it is possible that a good case may be made out for miscegenation. Race mixture has often accompanied or preceded cultural advance. Furthermore it has had the varied biological effects of widening the range of variability, of favoring the appearance of superior men through heterosis, and of making possible a multitude of fresh combinations of genetic factors which increase the versatility of the hereditary talent available in the population.[5]

The writers who insist upon the biological evil of the crossing of divergent races occasionally cite the unhappy conditions of the half-caste throughout the world as a confirmation of their general theories and of their lab-

---

3 *The Publications of the American Sociological Society,* vol. XIX, p. 53.
4 Op. cit., 343.
5 Idem, p. 348.

oratory experiments. The comparison because of its vivid concreteness appeals naturally to the average reader and to the proverbial man in the street. Yet it enjoys an extremely limited acceptance in scientific circles.

The condition of the half-caste throughout the world is, with some exceptions, deplorable. But the phenomenon can be explained without invoking a biological thesis. As Oldham wisely observed: "Half-castes are often the offspring of illicit unions and grow up without any real home. Their social environment is equally injurious both physically and morally; prejudice, hostility, and lack of opportunity stunt and warp their characters. Most serious of all perhaps is the extent to which a half-caste population is cut off from sharing in a natural tradition, which is one of the most powerful forces in creating stable character."[6] His observation furnishes a very plausible explanation of the condition of the Eurasians, the Mulattoes of South Africa, the Mestizos of the Philippines, and the half-breed American Indians. The social condition of the Mestizos in South America is probably superior to the condition of the other groups. That fact especially would seem to disprove the argument of the race purists because the Mestizos are to a large extent the offspring of formal marriages. Lord Brycc, a keen observer and student, has written, "What the ultimate effect of the intermixture of blood will have on the European element in Brazil, I will not venture to predict. If one may judge from a few remarkable cases it will not necessarily reduce the intellectual standard."[7]

It may be said likewise that no valid argument for either side of the question has been built upon the condition of the mulatto in the United States. This group though handicapped by some of the burdens which afflict the colored race enjoy a condition superior to that of the full-blooded Negro. Indeed, in this country there is a popular belief that the mulatto is superior to the full-

---

6 Oldham, op. cit., p. 147.

7 "South America Observations and Impressions," p. 477.

blooded Negro. But the belief is an unproved assumption. Social factors seem to explain adequately their condition. In the slave days the more attractive colored women were used as servants about the house. There they were brought into closer contact with the stream of social tradition and culture and were consequently better trained in the customs of the western civilization. Their offspring, in turn, because of appearance and possibly because of a paternal interest on the part of the master were given more attractive work about the house, and frequently they were taught trades. Consequently the mulattoes worked more efficiently and in turn were given even greater opportunities. They were furthermore assisted by an assumption current among white people that the mulattoes were more intelligent because of their white blood. This assumption acquired such force that even some sections of the colored race subscribed to it.[8]

Thus social forces can be recognized which would adequately explain both the superior achievement of the mulatto in the United States relative to the colored group and the deplorable condition of the Eurasian. Admittedly the existence of such forces does not necessarily exclude the influence of hereditary factors. It does, however, indicate the absence of any necessary causal relation beween the condition of the half-caste and the working of hereditary forces.

It seems prudent to conclude with Oldham, an unbiased student of race problems: "In regard to the biological effect of racial intermixture the result at which we arrive is that however definitely anthropologists and psychologists as the result of their studies may incline to one view or the other, the facts are still lacking on which an assured conclusion can be based."[9] That such a summary is not only a prudent but also an accurate statement of the present scientific attitude towards the problem is confirmed by a similar observation from another source. Professor Gregory, a strong opponent of

---

8 Cf. Reuter, "The Mulatto in the United States," pp. 181 sqq.
9 Op. cit., p. 148.

miscegenation, writes: "The doctrine of the inferiority of hybrids has not been established as a biological principle and there is much evidence against it."[10]

Here we might also advert to another argument against miscegenation, the psychological argument. It is founded upon the wide-spread aversion to interracial marriage prevalent among many people. This aversion is interpreted as a warning implanted by nature against the biological consequences of racial intermingling. It is regarded by some of the faithful as a natural expression of the commandment given to the Jews: "Let them marry to whom they will only so that it be to men of their own tribe."[11]

The practice of endogamy certainly has prevailed among many groups. Primitive tribes are usually opposed to marrying with tribes differing greatly from themselves. The ancient Greeks and the old Romans legislated against formal or legal marriages with other peoples. Among many of the modern Chinese and Russians a somewhat similar attitude is manifested. "Indeed we may say," writes Westermarck, "that probably every race considers it a disgrace if not a crime to marry with a very different race."[12]

In this case also there are many other factors which would adequately explain the wide-spread objection to such marriages without postulating the existence of an instinctive aversion. Among the Islamites, the Hindus, and the Jews, disparity of cult was a grave bar to intermarriage. Since religion and race were closely identified, interracial marriages were gradually forbidden. Among other groups other factors were at work. Aversion to the strange offspring probably influenced many. "And the children," moaned Esdras, "spoke half in the speech of Azotus and could not speak the Jewish language."[13] But the more prevalent factors are racial

---

10 "The Menace of Color," p. 234.
11 "Numbers," XXXVI, 7.
12 "The History of Human Marriage," vol. II, p. 41.
13 "The Book of Nehemius," XIII, v. 24.

pride and a sense of superiority. Practically every primitive tribe regards itself as being greatly superior to any other tribe, and a similar trait is manifested by modern nations.[14] "Those various influences," Oldham insists, "when combined and heightened by association and by an appeal to the deep-seated and powerful instinct which leads members of a community to defend even at the cost of their lives its existence and institutions, sufficiently explain the severity of the disapproval with which a society regards the marriage of its members with those who belong to a different community."[15] However, Westermarck though admitting racial pride as the dominant factor insists upon the existence of some sexual aversion akin to the instinctive feeling which deters animals of distinct species from pairing with each other.[16] Yet no modern psychologist of any standing would support his views.

Professor Dowd, an earnest student of race problems, has proposed an objection of a social nature. He contends that the high standards of living and of social practices which the whites have obtained would be lowered by intermarriage.[17] That the American Negro group live on a decidedly lower cultural plane than the white group is a fact which is above controversy. So, if the average Negro were to marry the average white person a general leveling process would probably follow. Yet that consequence would not follow in every actual case. Since the Negro culture in this country is identical in essence though not in quantity with that of the whites there are some Negroes who are undoubtedly superior to some of the whites. As Herskovits has observed, "Culture is transmitted not so much by physical heritage but by environment and social traditions. As we turn to Harlem we see in its social and political make-up a part of a larger city of the whole, separate from it but

14 Faris, *Institute of Pacific Relations,* preliminary paper.
15 Op. cit., p. 42.
16 Westermarck, op. cit., vol. II, p. 43.
17 "The Negro in American Life," ch. LX passim.

still essentially not different from any American city."[18] It is the same pattern but a different shade. Dowd's objection would not be applicable to every interracial marriage.

Moral Objections

Even though the biological and social evils of miscegenation have not been proved and are probably incapable of proof, a marriage between a Negro and a white person in the United States, at the present time, would place a considerable handicap on the moral life of the contracting parties. For that reason it would be wrong in an overwhelming number of cases for a member of either race to enter into an interracial marriage.

The average individual finds marriage an indispensable condition both for obtaining a reasonable amount of happiness and also for remaining faithful to the observance of the moral law. Yet not every haphazard marriage will serve as a means for the attainment of that end. Rather, though some latitude must be allowed for the working of that mysterious force which is called love, the contract must be made with a partner of such temperament and social position that they both may render mutual assistance and consolation to each other and that they both may live peacefully and contentedly. Young people act sinfully in neglecting in their selection of a partner to seek those personal traits and that social position which will furnish them a guarantee of a peaceful and compatible union during the long years of married life. They violate an obligation imposed by the fundamental virtue of prudence which obliges man in the important matters of life to use his most distinctive faculty, his reason, and to seek out and to follow the means best adapted for the attainment of his own welfare. They violate an obligation imposed by the virtue of piety, which obliges married people in so far as they are able, to create a home which will guarantee the physical and moral well-being of their children.

---

18 "The New Negro," p. 260.

If that principle is applied to the specific problem under consideration it would seem that, except in extraordinary cases, a marriage between a white person and a Negro is wrong. Such a marriage carries a strong presumption of having an unhappy ending, and it exposes the parties to the temptation of violating their marital obligations.

An indissoluble monogamous marriage is both a Christian ideal and a divine obligation. Yet in the United States such marriages are becoming rarer and more difficult of realization, even when the contracting parties are well mated and are members of the same race and class. Tainted by the spirit of the age, people have been rendered barren of the marital virtues, of the willingness to bear with weaknesses of the other party, of patience, of forbearance, of humility, of forgiveness, of the charity which thinketh no evil. Before marriage the defects of the other party are usually hidden by the veil which is quickly woven by the deft fingers of passion and infatuation. After a year or two of marital life that veil is usually rent, and the human weaknesses of each party stand out in cold reality. Then the parties are easily moved to anger, contempt, and regret; and because of the poverty of virtue such attacks are frequently fatal to the marriage bond and to the home. In every interracial marriage not only are those factors present but another handicap is added. Though infatuation may smother race prejudice during courtship, that antagonism may easily flare up after marriage and magnify petty differences during a moment of misunderstanding. It will render much more difficult the practice of forbearance, tolerance, and fidelity.

In many interracial marriages the sacrifices, which the contracting parties must make, are increased. Though their own racial feeling may be controlled they continue to live in a world where prejudice rages as a great reality. The social circle in which they moved formerly is in large measure closed to them. Social ostracism and isolation must be met with. They are forced more and more upon themselves with a consequent souring of disposition. Even contacts with relatives, which give solidity to some marriages, are rendered more difficult, and greater effort is made by the relatives to dissolve the alliance. Though regrettable it is nevertheless true that those who flout social prejudices must incur social penalties. Furthermore, the lives of the children are made more unpleasant. Each ancestral group may hesitate to admit them unreservedly to its fellowship. The children themselves may have some aversion toward the colored group and hatred toward the white group. In such offspring temptations to hatred of God and to despair are frequent. It was a mulatto who wrote; "I know why the caged bird beats its wing till its blood is red on the cruel bars."

Consequently, there is a strong presumption that an interracial marriage will have an unhappy ending and that its members are exposing themselves to the serious temptation to infidelity. Except in rare cases such marriages should be regarded as wrong.

In passing, advertence might be given to the possibilities of another argument suggested by Professor Miller. "To absorb a handful of Negroes in America," he writes, "and to leave the unbleached millions of Africa in their savage blackness would be to deepen the gulf of racial cleavage as a world problem. If there is any divine purpose working out the universal plan of racial amity and good-will throughout the world it would not be promoted by the immediate amalgamation either of the Negro or the Mongolian fragments now living in America."[19]

The objection may be raised that such marriages though carrying a presumption of unhappiness are desirable because of their ultimate effects, because such intermixture would soften the prejudice of this generation. Actually, the probability of extensive intermixture assuaging the present antagonisms is very remote. Let

---

19 *South Atlantic Quarterly*, vol. 25, p. 245.

the admission be made that a group of each race by being brought into intimate contact might acquire a mutual sympathy, a fuller understanding of their similar natures, and that deeper knowledge which is fatal to intolerance. Nevertheless, any noticeable increase in the numbers of such alliances would occasion a fresh outbreak of racial hatred. Devotees of racial purity would become alarmed and the relatives of the parties to such contracts might attempt vengeance upon the entire colored group because of an imagined disgrace. Parents fearing that their children might contract racial marriages would seek more extensive segregation. Dowd states that the Philadelphia riot of 1849 was occasioned by the marriage of a white man to a colored woman.[20]

Furthermore, it is wrong to permit couples to expose themselves to such serious spiritual dangers for the purpose of diminishing prejudice when other untried means exist. Untried means do exist. The resources of religion and education as methods of dispelling prejudices have never been adequately mined. Even experiments in these fields are preferable since the cost of an occasional failure would not be borne by a few individuals. Later, when the prejudice has been partially discarded and when the evil consequences of such marital unions would be less, intermarriage may be permitted. But to invoke intermarriage at the present time as a means of dissolving prejudice would be to use not only a questionable means but one disproportionate to the end.

The Teachings of the Church and the Theologians

Much of the discussion in the preceding paragraphs has been based upon general moral principles. It may be interesting, however, to examine the official attitude of the Catholic Church. Though earnestly urging her members to respect and reverence the civil law, the Church does not regard as invalid properly solemnized marriages between Negroes and whites who are subject

---

20 Op. cit., p. 446.

to her jurisdiction.[21] Of that fact there is no question. But aside from a clear position on that point, her attitude toward the other marital implications of the American race problem must, in the absence of definite pronouncements, be construed from her general teaching. Since the primary purpose of marriage is the procreation and the education of children, she opposes usually any marriage of which the offspring would be physically weak. That attitude explains in part her insistence upon the impediment of consanguinity and also her protest against the use of marriage by those afflicted with social diseases. Hence if the physical weakness of the half-caste was definitely proved, the Church would strongly oppose interracial marriages.

The Church has not accepted the thesis of the inferiority of the hybrid, nor has she acquiesced in the contention that the white race is the superior race,[22] nor has she refused to solemnize marriages between the members of different races or classes. Records are extant which indicate that as early as the fifth century the Church assumed a definite attitude. Though the Church accepted in large measure the civil laws of the Roman Empire and though those laws were used as a model and nucleus of ecclesiastical legislation, the Church cancelled and condemned that ancient legislation of the Roman Empire and of the Teutonic nations which forbade marriages between different races and different classes of society.[23] Her attitude in modern times is perhaps best summarized by the eminent canonist, Wernz: "The Church does not oppose the valid and licit celebration of marriage between free persons because of the disparity of nature or of nobility; neither does she deny legitimacy to the offspring. Even though some equality of condition between the partners is most desirable, too great care in avoiding every disparity is

21 Slater, "Questions of Moral Theology," p. 260. Cf. Fallon, "Eugenics."
22 Acta Apostolicae Sedis, March, 1926. "De Missionibus,"
23 "Corpus Juris," 12 c XXXII, q. 2.

foreign to the mind of the Church which rather strives to coordinate all men into the one family of the Heavenly Father."[24]

To a large extent those general statements have reference or application only to the objective validity of marriage and are representative of the ideals of the Church. In every marital contract there are many other factors involved beside the objective validity of the marriage; for example, the peculiar dispositions of the contracting parties, their compatibility, their economic and social position. These factors can influence the marriage so drastically that its moral character may be definitely altered. Since these factors vary widely and since they are frequently affected by the customs and circumstances of a locality they are not usually considered in the judgment of the Church on the moral character of any marriage. Such a decision is left to the theologians who are more familiar with local conditions and who in their systematized treatises on the duties of the individual would naturally give consideration to such a problem. In the writings of the theologians one may seek knowledge of the attitude of the Church toward a problem, just as one may seek in the writings of Blackstone or Marshall the attitude of the civil law towards a definite situation.

But the specific question of the advisability of marriages between blacks and whites in the United States has not been discussed by the modern theologians. Like other writers, their attention is generally occupied by those problems which are pressingly acute for a large number of people. Nevertheless, in the writings of the older and more prominent theologians there may be found a discussion about the morality of a somewhat similar type of marriage—the marriage between the peasant and the noble in Europe. Their attitude toward such a marriage suggests the probable nature of their reaction to unions between blacks and whites.

---

24 "Jus Decretalium," vol. II, p. 380.

The older theologians admitted the absence of anything inherently wrong in the marriage between a peasant and a noble. Yet, because of the grave probability of quarrels and regrets on the part of the bride and of the groom and because of the shame and dishonor felt by the relatives, such marriages were often regarded as illicit. Sanchez, an eminent ecclesiastical writer of the sixteenth century, thought that the engagement which preceded such a type of marriage was invalid and that the parents acted properly if they appealed to the civil magistrate to prevent the completion of the alliance.[25] St. Alphonsus, a distinguished theologian of the eighteenth century, thought that a member of the nobility sinned by marrying a peasant because of the disgrace which he brought upon his family and because of the antagonisms which he occasioned by his action.[26] The spirit of that teaching may still be found in the writings of modern theologians and canonists. It is taught that any substantial change in the social condition of one party to an engagement furnishes a just occasion for the dissolution of the engagement contract because such disparity makes for unhappiness. Theologians, also, hold that a notable disparity of condition is a reasonable cause for objection on the part of the parents.[27] If, for these reasons, a marriage between a peasant and a noble was thought to be improper and to some extent sinful, then, it would seem that the theologians would be forced, *a fortiori,* to extend the same teaching to marriages between blacks and whites.

II. Social Separation

If it is recognized that certain types of valid marriages are undesirable because of a strong presumption that they will be unsuccessful and spiritually dangerous, it must be also admitted that proportionate means should

---

25 Sanchez, "De Sancto Matrimonii Sacramento Disputationum," lib. I, disp. 14, n. 3.
26 "Theologia Moralis," lib. 6, tr. 6, n. 851.
27 Capello, "De Sacrementis," vol. III, p. 92.

be taken to protect imprudent and thoughtless young people from contracting such marriages. Such is the dictate of prudence. To prevent marriages in the United States between blacks and whites new means need be devised. Such marriages are rare, partly because of prejudice, partly because of social separation. The question, then, which remains for discussion is to what extent should those factors be continued as means of preventing interracial marriages?

No difficulty is presented by racial prejudice. As observed elsewhere it is something which is evil in itself and which actually creates the undesirableness of such marital contracts. As racial prejudice diminishes, the objection to such a marriage also diminishes. Any action or movement which offers genuine promise of lessening racial prejudice deserves unreserved support. Marriages between blacks and whites are not intrinsically wrong.

The phenomenon of social separation possesses a different character. If the term is properly restricted such separation does not constitute to any appreciable extent the cause of the objection to such contracts. Neither does it accentuate racial prejudice. Rather any sudden attempt to abolish the separation of the races would increase the prejudice because of the attitude of the community. Nevertheless, social separation is regarded by many as a flagrant violation of the ethics of Christ.

The term 'social separation' in this essay is intended to designate the separation of the races in those circumstances and activities in which friendships conducive to marriage might naturally be formed. The term is not designed to include the separation of the races in trains, schools, business offices, and industrial plants. The disjoining of the races under those circumstances might more properly be dsignated as segregation. The ethical implications of segregation will be discussed in the next chapter. A justification of those forms of separation, if possible, must rest upon grounds other than those of being conducive to interracial marriage. No necessary connection exists between marriage and contacts in trains, schools, and factories. The young men and young women of this generation meet in innumerable places; in transportation vehicles, in shops, in offices, in universities. For the normal case, the acquaintance formed under such circumstances develops into that deeper friendship and intimacy conducive to marriage only when the young people may meet socially; only when they may be invited to the homes of one another; only when the partner of one is acceptable to the friends of the other. The scions of the wealthy have contact with the poor in business relations but marriages between those classes are exceptional because they do not meet socially. The Jew and the Gentile have contact in educational institutions and yet marriages are infrequent because of the social barriers raised by each group. Likewise, if the Negroes and the whites are separated socially, interracial marriages are placed beyond the realm of probability.

With that definition in mind the question may be asked whether social separation is justifiable. Are the persons whose actions render the existing separation possible acting according to Christian standards? The answer has been partly implied in the opening paragraph of this section. If the undesirableness of black and white marriages is admitted then proportionate means should be taken to prevent such marriages. The means in turn are justifiable provided that they do not conflict with any precept of the moral law.

Relative to the former provision the objection has been made that social separation is entirely unnecessary. It is maintained that if racial prejudice possesses the force attributed to it the races may indulge in complete social intermingling without the slightest probability of interracial marriages being formed. Truly racial prejudice would keep many members of one race from entering into any marital contract with members of the other race. Yet it should be noted that the full-blooded Negroes who might have entrée to a white social group would be free from many of those negative factors which invigorate prejudice, such as ignorance, poverty, and unrefinement. In such instances the consciousness of mutual interests could easily neutralize the aversion. But the more practical case is that of the mulatto. Many mulattoes of both sexes are, by white standards, very comely and attractive. Marriages between that group of the colored population of the United States and the whites would probably be more frequent if the races mingled socially.

Relative to the latter provision social separation as a means of preventing interracial marriages could contravene the moral law by being either unjust or uncharitable. Occasionally the question of the injustice of this practice has been raised.[28] Yet if the various forms of separation which have been designated as segregation are excluded it is extremely difficult to distinguish in the issue any elements of strict justice. In fact the theologians have found the analysis of any form of social discrimination in terms of justice to be a very elusive task. It is a problem about which a wide-spread difference of opinion exists.[29] The more pertinent objections are those raised by many modern writers who by furious excoriations denounce social separation as a flagrant violation of Christ's commandment of brotherly love. Attention is directed by those writers to the offense which the Negroes suffer as a consequence of the practice. Then the conclusion is drawn that the practice must be wrong. For offending a neighbor is the antithesis of loving him.

The Christian Teaching About the Morality of Social Contacts

To limit intimate friendships to members of a small group, to confine social relations to members of a definite class, and to co-operate in other social discriminations from which people occasionally take offense are practices which in the opinion of the world conflict seriously

---

28 Cf. Dubois, "Darkwater," passim.
29 Cf. *Irish Theological Quarterly*, vol. II, pp. 70-84, and pp. 242-249.

with the ideal of human brotherhood as preached by Christ. They are practices which contravene the ideal of social democracy. Yet admitting their unidealistic character, it does not follow that such practices are morally wrong. It does not follow that because they give offense to certain individuals they are forbidden to the Christian under pain of sin. Social separation is not seriously uncharitable because some members of the colored group are offended by the practice.

Evidently, wide-spread misunderstanding exists about the extent of the Christian's obligation to love his neighbor. Consequently, before entering upon a discussion of the alleged uncharitableness of social separation it may be advisable to examine several fundamental principles which are indispensable if one is to acquire an accurate and thorough knowledge of Christian teaching; if one is to attempt to pass judgment upon the consistency between the belief of the Christian and his practice. The Christian in his interpretation of various texts of the Scripture and in his application of the teachings of Christ to the ever-changing social conditions is influenced not by emotion but by well defined principles. Indeed, the existence and influence of such principles seem to be unknown to many of the writers who accuse the white group of uncharitableness. Their concept of Christianity seems to be based upon a few isolated biblical texts. They regard the practice of Christianity as the adoption of an emotional, unreasoned attitude toward all activities of life.

Knowledge of the distinction between matters of precept and matters of counsel is of the nature of a first principle of Christianity and essential for the acquisition of even an elementary understanding of its doctrine. Not all of Christ's sermons and instructions were the expressions of commandments or of obligatory rules of life. When Christ spoke, He often emphasized the ten commandments and occasionally promulgated a new precept. But more frequently, He gave expression to an ideal mode of life which His disciples were exhorted to follow. So in an examination of the sermons recorded in the gospel, care must be taken to distinguish the expression of an ideal of life from the commandments which were imposed under penalty of sin. Though a Christian may fail to rise to the highest ideal he does not thereby violate a commandment.

The validity of this distinction has been challenged. Yet the gospel texts furnish abundant evidence that Christ wished His listeners to make such a distinction. The instance of the young man asking, "What good shall I do that I may have life everlasting?" is one striking illustration. The apostles and the early Christian fathers who were unquestionably competent to bear witness to the true meaning of Christ's teaching insisted upon its observance.[30] Since then the distinction has been consistently emphasized by the theologians and other teachers of the Church in their interpretation of the Scriptures. Moreover, even if such authoritative confirmation was lacking, reason would vindicate the validity of the distinction. Unless it is admitted the alternative must be faced that all men are bound to distribute all their wealth to the poor, that all men are bound to live celibate lives. Unless the distinction is granted it must be recognized that an overwhelming number of Christians in every generation have failed to comply with the precepts of their great spiritual Leader. Yet the admission must also be made that knowledge of the distinction is one thing and its application to certain biblical texts is another. Without the aid of authoritative teaching it is, at times, unquestionably difficult to construe whether the words of the text should be understood as a precept or as a counsel.

In the presence of such a difficulty one criterion by which the counsel may be distinguished from the precept is the incapacity of the action to be translated into an obligatory norm of conduct for all men. Christ, being Divine, would not impose upon His followers obligatory

---

30 Cf. Bouquillon, "Theologia Moralis Fundamentalis," p. 243.

rules of conduct which conflicted and disturbed the divinely established order of nature. Christ, being all wise, would not oblige the masses of His followers to perform actions which consistently surpassed the powers of the average individual; actions which men of all ages would regard as unreasonable if imposed on all men indiscriminately. Bouquillon, an eminent American theologian of the last generation, has taught that Christ added few new precepts to the natural law; that for the most part, His sermons were but a more definite pronouncement of the natural law.[31] Hence, since the discriminating norm of the natural law is rational human nature, the accuracy of any interpretation of a commandment is indicated, to a large extent, by its reasonableness, by its conformity with rational human nature.

If these principles are applied to the teaching of Christ it becomes evident that Christ did not prohibit every action which could give offense to any person or group. Much of His teaching, as it has been taught through the centuries, was but a matter of counsel, the recommendation of a field in which the fervent Christian could strive to acquire perfection. In the world live many supersensitive persons who take offense at the most innocent incidents. If a man's actions were to be constantly conditioned by the feelings of such people he would be placed in a persistent state of inhibition. What is forbidden, then, is the placing of an action which would give reasonable offense.

The term "reasonable offense" may appear to some to be vague and arbitrary. Yet in traditional Christian thought rather definite limitations are placed upon its meaning. Consequently, in order that an accurate impression may be obtained of its scope, it may be helpful to examine even in greater detail the traditional theological doctrine which treats of man's obligation to his neighbor. To some readers, this extensive discussion of authoritative Christian teaching relative to charity may

---

31 Bouquillon, op. cit., p. 82.

seem abnormal and disproportionate. Yet it seems appropriate because of the abnormal confusion and misunderstanding existing about the point in question.

In the teaching of the theologians the primary emphasis is placed upon an internal act of love toward all mankind. That internal disposition need be translated into action only on the occasion of a specific temptation or contact. If a neighbor in need is encountered, then assistance must be given, provided that the individual's personal needs have been proportionately provided for. All direct actions of hatred and malice are, of course, proscribed. But beyond giving assistance to the needy and the avoiding of positive and obvious acts of ill will the theologians are reluctant to impose further obligations. Usually they content themselves with obliging the individual to perform those actions, the omission of which would indicate hatred or contempt.

In the technical language of the Schoolmen the individual is usually bound to show only the "communia signa delectionis," those indications of good-will, those civilities which one citizen shows to another, which one relative shows to another.[32] Their interpretation is reasonable and harmonizes with the capacity of the average individual. All signs of hostility are forbidden and the mutual exchange of civilities gives evidence of the acceptance of the doctrine of human brotherhood. On the other hand, the individual is not so thoroughly burdened with concern for his fellowman that opportunity and energy for other activities is denied to him. Considerable latitude is given to the individual to develop friendships with those whose natures and tastes harmonize best with his own. Especially it should be noted that the theologians ordinarily do not hold that a Christian is obliged to manifest to all men special signs of friendships, such as inviting an acquaintance to dinner or to his home. Such signs, as Aquinas observed centures ago in his Summa, indicate a special familiarity or special in-

---

32 Noldin, "Summa Theologiae Moralis," vol. II, p. 97. Ballerini-Palmieri, "Opus Theologicum Morale," vol. II, pp. 130-134.

timacy and are due to no one.[33] Insistence upon the extension of such favors to all with whom one might have contact with during life would place an insurmountable burden upon the shoulders of the Christian. However, the Christian who strives to follow the Master most closely will show special attention to the poor, the friendless, and the social outcast. But offense taken on account of their omission should be attributed not to uncharitableness but to unreasonable sensitiveness.

The Racial Application of the Traditional Teaching

If this Christian tradition is applied to the specific phase of racial contacts under consideration it appears evident that many of the actions involved in social separation are not immoral. If offense should be taken by any members of the colored group as a consequence of these actions it would seem to be unwarranted. For many of the acts involved, such as the failure to extend an invitation to dinner or to a private social or to one's home, comprise merely a denial of the "specialia signa delectionis." These signs of special friendship are usually due to no one. Professor Kelly Miller has written; "If the members of one race prefer to limit household intercourse and pleasurable intimacies to their own group there can be no reasonable grounds for complaint."[34]

However, the admission must be made that in the practice of social separation even the "communia signa" are occasionally denied to the Negroes. For example, invitations to social events of a semi-official nature are not extended at times to the colored group. Among the white group those invitations would be regarded as "communia signa" and the failure to extend them to a white person would be viewed as cause for reasonable offense. But even in some of those instances the practice seems justifiable. The actions involved have no

---

33 Summa Theologica, 2a., 2ae., q. 25, a. 9.

34 "The Negro in New England," June, 1926, in the *Harvard Graduate Magazine*.

value in themselves (for it may be assumed that the people are not in dire need of food) except in as far as they denote good-will and a desire to promote the happiness of another. In most instances they achieve their objective. In this particular instance they would probably lead to interracial marriages and in turn bring much unhappiness to both groups. In no true sense would they symbolize good-will; and both the colored and white groups if genuinely concerned about the well-being of the other group should desire their exclusion.

The acknowledgment of the existence of a group of common signs which though due to members of the white group may not be extended to the members of the colored group suggests the wisdom of another admission. While the relation of certain personal contacts with marriage is clear and while in other contacts the absence of any relation is equally evident, there exists a vague border zone between the two groups of contacts and the actions involved in that field offer, especially in the North, many difficulties. Above the Mason and Dixon line "socials" are frequently conducted by organizations in which both black and white have membership. Will intermarriage follow because both groups attend those semi-public functions? Apparently not if both groups attend in sufficient numbers to associate among themselves. However, the line should be drawn, it seems, in such contacts as dancing. Both groups might attend a public banquet without any violation of the principle.

In certain sections of India a custom is reported to prevail which might possibly be adopted as a temporary adjustment to our difficult race problem. There, the men of one caste may visit the men of the other caste, and likewise the women of various castes may exchange visits, but the men and women of different castes never meet socially. Hence, marriages between castes seldom occur. In like manner the colored and white men might dine together or visit one another without any violation of the principle. If the women teachers of a public school have a "social" there is no reason why the colored teachers should be excluded. If the male employees of a factory have an outing there is no reason why the colored workmen should be excluded. In fact, failure to invite or to accept a colored person under those circumstances would give, it seems, reasonable cause for offense and would constitute a sin against charity.

Throughout this entire chapter an attempt has been made to show that social separation is justifiable and compatible with Christianity. Only cursory instances of the practice have been suggested. In concrete circumstances the individual must determine when the races should remain apart. But the individual should not forget that the mere entrance of a Negro as an equal into a white man's home does not constitute a breach of the principle. The harmful contacts are those between men and women of marriageable age. Other domestic contacts, if prudently regulated, may be helpful as a means of increasing sympathy and understanding between the races. Moreover, though social separation may be justifiable, many Christians sin in the means which they use to secure it. When it is found necessary the Christian should act with love, with humility, with the genuine gentleness which characterized every action of the Master. If there existed both a mutual understanding of the principle involved and also a genuine Christian wish to avoid giving offense, many embarrassing situations could be avoided.

It should be noted that the phrase "social separation" has been used rather than the phrase "social equality" to describe the problems discussed in this section. The latter term conveys a false concept. The separation of the colored and white groups in social relations does not imply the superiority of the white group. The Jews are not superior to the Gentiles because they oppose interracial marriages. What has lead to the use of the term is an assumption prevalent among many whites that the Negroes seek social contact with them. The Negroes desire equality of opportunity with the white Americans in politics, in education, and in industry, but social intercourse is regarded by a large number of them as a different matter. Actually the colored person who attempts social intermingling with white people is often disgraced among his own group. Dr. Herskovits has written, "I, myself, have observed that there is a pressure within the Negro community against associating with whites which parallels that in the white group with regard to the Negroes."[35]

---

35 *Current History*, p. 902, Sept., 1926.

CHAPTER VI

SEGREGATION

In the preceding chapter social separation was discussed in so far as it is reasonably conducive to interracial marriages. In this chapter and the subsequent two, attention will be given to the separation of the races in other phases of life, the justification of which must be founded upon some other basis than that of the undesirability of miscegenation. These separations ramify into all the activities of life and range from the separation of the races in schools, trains, and residential districts, by law, to the exclusion of the Negro from restaurants, theatres, and factories by the prejudicial attitude of employers, employees, and patrons. A logical division of these various forms of separations is extremely difficult because of the overlapping. Yet in the popular mind the forms of separation effected by law are frequently designated as segregation, while those effected by individual initiative are described as discriminations. Such an arrangement and use of terms is not entirely accurate, but because of its wide acceptance it will be observed in this essay. A study will be attempted of the three forms of segregation most widely discussed; for, segregation in trains, in schools, and in residential sections.

I. Segregation in Trains

In all the Southern States, except Missouri, the railroads are obliged by law to furnish separate accomodations for Negroes and whites. In many of these States, street cars and steamboats are subject to similar legislation. The separate compartments must be by law "equal to comfort" and the conductors are instructed to assign each passenger to his respective compartment, and the passenger is obliged to take the seat assigned. Exceptions are made for servants and prisoners.

These laws have a relatively recent origin, having been promulgated for the most part between 1880 and 1910. One probable reason for their absence earlier than that date is, as Johnson observed, that "railroad travel was not so prevalent at an earlier period as it is at the present and the colored population lacked both means and motive for extended and frequent use of the railroads."[1] Another reason was that some of the early railroads carried first- and second-class coaches and most of the Negroes rode second-class. The dropping of the second-class coaches on the main lines made the problem more acute. While restrictive legislation relative to segregation in common carriers is at the present time confined to the Southern States it is interesting to note that the legal justification of such a procedure originated in the North. As early as 1867, the Negroes were segregated in Pennsylvania by at least one railroad, the West Chester Railway Company. The practice of that railroad was attacked by the Negroes and the Abolitionists, and an appeal was made to the courts of that State. But the courts declared that the practice was in accordance with law and stated, "It is much wiser to avert the consequences of this repulsion of race by separation than to punish afterwards the breach of peace it may have caused."[2] Though the practice was later abandoned in the North, it spread rapidly in the South, and laws were enacted by the various commonwealths making the separation obligatory. The Negroes, of course, protested against these statutes and stigmatized them as unconstitutional. In 1896, in the famous case of Pleesy v. Ferguson, the statutes were attacked before the Supreme Court of the United States. That Court, however, adopting to a large extent the decisions of the courts of Pennsylvania, held the

---

1 Johnson, "The Development of State Legislation Concerning the Free Negro," p. 151.

2 *The Illinois Law Review*, vol. XXI, p. 706, March, 1927.

statutes to be constitutional and to be a valid exercise of the police power. The same decision has been frequently reaffirmed and approved.[3] Therefore any discussion of the morality of these laws must revolve on the question whether any natural right of the Negro is violated by such legislation.

The wrongs, which the Negro claims to suffer as a censequence of these laws, may be divided into two categories: those which are due to a defective and partial enforcement and those which are inherent in the laws themselves. Abstracting, for the present, from the former let us examine the morality of the laws in themselves.

The Morality of Legal and Theoretical Segregation

In order that the opinions advanced here may be placed in their true perspective, we would remind the reader that in this section the discussion treats of the law alone. Wrongs which are attributable to defective enforcement—and their number is numerous—are to be examined in subsequent sections. We would also remind the reader that here there is no question of the unidealistic character of segregation. Segregation undoubtedly stands in stark opposition to the ideals of Christ and to the ideal of the brotherhood of man. Segregation is regrettable, undesirable, a practice which should be abolished as soon as it may be done without creating a worse situation. Segregation is an institution which, though affording the colored group a few temporary advantages, has occasioned wide-spread wrongs. Yet just as the wrong of drinking intoxicating liquors does not necessarily follow from the abuses involved in the liquor traffic, in like manner, the wrong of segregation does not follow necessarily from the evils involved in its practice. So the questions may be asked: Is segregation not only an evil but also an injustice? Do the laws, as they stand on the statute books, necessarily violate a strict right of the Negro?

---

[3] U. S. Reports, vol. 163, p. 537, and vol. 245, p. 61, Oct. Term, 1917.

The Negroes protest that their rights to liberty and honor are transgressed by such legislation. A considerable freedom of action is, of course, indispensable for reasonable living. Yet Christian teachers also maintain that the State may restrict the liberty of individuals in so far as the common good demands.[4] Actually, every government without protest from the thoughtful citizens limits the freedom of its subjects in numerous respects, by traffic regulation and by restrictions placed upon the operation of certain kinds of business. These restrictions become unjust only when they are unnecessary for the promotion of the common good or when they place too great a burden upon one group of citizens.

Are such restrictions necessary in the South? The reply to that inquiry may be drawn from an examination of the effects of an attempt on the part of the State to enforce immediately a contrary practice. If the laws were immediately abrogated and if an effort were made to guarantee to the Negro the civil right of using jointly with the whites a Southern railroad coach, the public peace would most probably be gravely disturbed.

The overwhelming majority of white people in the South would fiercely oppose, at the present time, any innovation which would bring the Negroes into close and prolonged contact with themselves. Their objection would be due, partly to a natural opposition to any change in the established order, partly to fierce racial hatred and prejudice, and partly to the physical discomfort which they would suffer. Unquestionably the average white person reared in the South would suffer considerable discomfort if he were forced to ride for several hours in a Southern railroad coach, a fair proportion of whose occupants were Negroes. That sense of discomfort could easily electrify a prejudice which otherwise might remain dormant. The mere entrance of a Negro would frequently be a signal for a grave disturbance of the public peace. Such a disturbance in other sections of the country could be controlled easily

[4] Cathrein, "*Philosophia Moralis,*" n. 540.

by the officials and the police. But in the Southern States not only would the average white citizen fail to co-operate in an effort to restore peace and to guarantee to the Negro his place in the train, but the officials and police because of their manifest sympathies would connive in the actions of the populace. The Negroes, on the other hand, if they were present in sufficiently large numbers, might insist upon entering. The grave consequences of such an action are obvious.

A most significant indication that separation is indispensable may be found in the unanimous attitude of Southerners toward the institution. In other matters in which more vital rights of the Negro are involved, there may be found in the South a considerable group of influential citizens who insist upon the recognition of the Negro's rights. Despite the activities of powerfully organized minorities of race fanatics, such as the Klan, there are whites who try to secure from the State protection of the Negro's life and health, and the bestowal of equal facilities of education on both races. Many others, though inactive, recognize the reasonableness of such actions. Yet the Southern attitude toward segregation is still so strongly entrenched, that not one white citizen of influence has challenged the necessity of the separation in common carriers. To advocate the abolition of such segregation immediately would be to sponsor legislation which would carry a presumption of invalidity. Usually if a law is to be valid it must be capable of a reasonable degree of enforcement.[5]

By the abolition of segregation in the South, the rougher elements of both races would be brought together. The joining of those sections of both races in such close and prolonged contact might easily create at the present time a situation which would make traveling very unpleasant. Neither would the white group be entirely responsible for such a situation. A Negro of prominence wrote some years ago: "White people,

[5] Bouquillon, "Theologia Moralis Fundamentalis," p. 110.

however, are not entirely to blame for the bringing about of these conditions in the South. Rowdy Negroes often board the trains full of bad liquor and bent upon a fight. They sit down and drink more whiskey, lurch through the car, insult respectable colored women and men, and make themselves not only nuisances but positively dangerous. It is no wonder that white Southern legislatures have sought by prohibitive laws to protect their own men and women from such disgusting and dangerous displays of black savagery as this.''[6] That description applies only to a small fraction of the colored group. Yet it has value because it illustrates vigorously the occasions for racial quarrels which could arise if the black and the whites were to ride in the same coaches in the South at the present time.

In the interests of public comfort and public peace the separation of the races in the South seems permissible, at least in theory, for the State possesses the power of enacting whatever measures are deemed necessary for the public peace. The necessity for such regulations in States, such as Mississippi and Alabama, is unquestionable. In other States, such as Virginia, the need is not so clear, but the presumption for the validity of such a law is with the State.[7] The regulations which apply to electric cars are less excusable, since the length of the contact is shorter and the inconvenience is less.

Neither in theory is the colored group burdened with greater restrictions. Liberty of action is limited for both. The whites are forbidden to enter the colored coach, and the colored are forbidden to enter the white coach. To both races equal accomodations are guaranteed by law.

The contention is made that such legislation violates the Negro's right to honor and respect and places a badge of inferiority upon him. Yet in theory the separation, apart from concrete circumstances, does not appear to be derogatory. It implies physical differences but not

---

6 Corrothers, ''In Spite of the Handicap,'' p. 120.

7 Cf. Ryan, ''Declining Liberty,'' p. 55.

the superiority of one race over the other. The separation of men and women in public waiting rooms does not connote the superiority of one sex over the other. The Supreme Court observed in the famous Pleesy v. Ferguson Case: "We consider the underlying fallacy of the plaintiff's argument to consist in the assumption that the enforced separation of the two races stamps the colored race with a badge of inferiority. If that be so it is not by reason of anything found in the act but solely because the colored race choose to put that construction upon it."[8]

Justice Harlan in a dissenting opinion to that case asked if it were not derogatory to the Negro why should not the State separate Catholics from Protestants on the trains. The answer given was that the prejudice between those groups did not threaten the public peace and comfort as did the prejudice against the Negro. The differences existing between a large section of the colored population and the white race is striking and to a certain extent unparalleled by the differences existing between the white Americans and any other group, such as the European immigrants, the Indians, or the Chinese. The Negro, in physical features, is much different from the white man. Constituting a larger percentage of the population of the Southern States than the Oriental or the Indian does in Western sections he presents a more practical problem. Two business partners or roommates will occasionally recognize that their temperaments are imcompatible and agree to separate. The one does not feel himself inferior to the other. Lot separated from Abraham without consciousness of being degraded. So in view of the strong racial feeling in the South the segregation of the races on common carriers does not seem to be immoral. There is another ethical objection, namely, that which is founded upon the contention that inferior accommodations always accompany segregation. That objection will be examined in our dis-

[8] U. S. Reports, vol. 163, p. 537.

cussion of the abuses involved in the enforcement of the laws.

The question may be asked: If segregation on Southern trains is justifiable, why should not the practice be introduced into the North? The answer is, segregation in the North is unnecessary. The Negroes do not dwell there proportionately in such great numbers, segregation is not a custom or tradition, and the prejudice is not so deeply rooted. Restrictions upon the liberty of the individual are justifiable only when they are necessary for the promotion of the common good. In the North, any attempted restriction in common carriers could not be justified as a necessary means of ensuring public peace, for the police officials have proved themselves competent, with a few exceptions, to subdue the disturbances which have arisen. Neither could the practice be justified as a means of increasing the public comfort or the public good. Usually an attempt to introduce new forms of segregation in the North results in a disturbance. The colored group is naturally antagonized, and the thoughts of the white group are turned to the fact of racial differences and they try to extend the racial line even further.[9] Hence, any attempt to separate the Negroes from the whites in the trains or the public conveyances of the North would be unjustified and would clearly violate a right of the Negro. In the South, decidedly different conditions prevail. Separation has been an established custom, and any effort to uproot it completely and drastically would fan into a flame the smoldering embers of racial hatred. It has been a scaffolding which permitted the two races in a difficult situation to live together and to pursue their respective ends. Such laws, though deplorable, are not always unjust. Racial feeling has not sufficiently abated to justify any agitation for its complete repeal.

---

9 Cf. "The Negro in Chicago," p. 626.

The Injustice of the Existing Segregation

The Negro does suffer numerous and extensive injuries because of the failure of the various States to enforce equitably all the provisions of the law. While on some lines and in some railroad stations the accommodations given to the Negro are absolutely identical with those furnished to the whites, it is equally true that the accommodations accorded the Negroes on other trains are decidedly inferior. Dr. Woofter writes: "Most railroads herd them into half coaches which are part colored passenger coach and part baggage car. Often there is only one toilet for both sexes and sometimes the conductor, brakeman, or news' butcher makes his headquarters in the colored compartment forcing colored passengers to stand. Sometimes they are furnished wooden coaches which are dangerously sandwiched between the heavy steel coaches."[10] Mrs. Hammond testifies to the same facts, and Professor Dowd states that such conditions prevail at least on the branch lines.[11]

Such treatment of the colored people by the railroads is unquestionably a grave injustice. On the part of the railroad company it constitutes a form of extortion or profiteering, since the same fare is collected from both races, and since the fare exacted from the whites is presumably a just return for the services rendered. Neither is the objection of the railroads pertinent that because of the expense involved in providing separate compartments they could not afford to furnish equal accommodations to the blacks. If the revenue is insufficient the rates should be raised. To insist that the Negroes, the weaker group, should bear the expense of such a public policy and the expense of superior accommodations offered to the whites is a species of injustice which rivals in boldness the acts of the great tyrants of history.

The failure of the railroads to provide sleeping and parlor cars, for the colored group, constitutes another

---

10 Woofter, "The Basis of Racial Adjustment," p. 239.

11 Hammond, "In Black and White," p. 239. Dowd, "The Negro in American Life," p. 111.

injustice. During this generation to deny such service to a person of refinement subjects him to serious inconvenience. Mrs. Hammond, a Southern woman, maintains that the number of Negroes who would use these services is much greater than the people imagine. At least as she suggests the number would warrant the hauling of Pullmans for the colored several times during the week.[12] If on the other hand the number of Negroes seeking those services should be small the carrying of them in the white Pullmans would not constitute an inconvenience. The danger of any disturbance to the public peace should in this case be relatively less since the people who can afford extra services should be capable of greater self-restraint. The objection to the presence of a few Negroes in a Pullman is unreasonable. At any rate an injustice is involved in the present arrangement because the colored have by law a right to equal accommodations.

Another gross abuse involved in the admininstration of the laws is the discourteous treatment accorded to the colored. "The administration of segregation regulations by minor functionaries," writes Woofter, "who are often prejudiced and brutal toward the weaker race is an additional source of irritation to the Negro. In the hands of ignorant and prejudiced employees segregation can be made a smarting insult."[13] Corrothers graphically stated in his description of a steamboat journey from Washington: "A white person who unthinkingly crosses the invisible dead line is corrected apologetically by the steamboat watchman; a Negro who ignorantly does so is stormed at profanely."[14]

Such treatment is neither characteristic of all railroads nor is it necessarily inherent in the system. Yet when these insults are added to the inferior accommodations and the restrictions placed by law, a condition is created which makes traveling for the Negro most un-

---

12 Op. cit., p. 81.
13 Op. cit., p. 239.
14 Op. cit., p. 118.

pleasant and trying. That condition constitutes, to our mind, the most serious ethical objection to segregation and deprives the practice of much of the justification which it enjoys in theory. The fact that a few roads treat the Negro equitably indicates that an equitable segregation is possible. The fact that most roads capitalize the Negro's weaknesses raises a reasonable doubt against the practicability of an equitable segregation. Hence, if the existing segregation in common carriers is to be regarded as anything but wrong and sinful, and if Southern whites are to escape the stigma of co-operating in a sinful and disgusting mistreatment of a weaker group, then an immediate effort must be made by those in authority to correct these glaring abuses. Neither should the members of the white group forget the existence of a very strong presumption that the law will never be fairly enforced. Oldham observed: . "The white race enjoy almost a complete monopoly of political power and to act justly in such circumstances demands a degree of virtue which the average human nature has hardly attained. The world has recognized in regard to individuals that it is not right or possible for a man to be judge in his own cause."[15]

The responsibility for such injustices rests primarily upon the railroad corporations who fail to render to the Negro the comfort, the service, and the elementary courtesy to which he has a strict right. Hence, the officials of those companies sin seriously. But an almost equal share of the responsibility rests upon the public officials of the city, the county, and the state in which such conditions prevail. They fail to enforce the law equitably; they are false to a most sacred and fundamental function of government, that of protecting the weak. The individual voter in those States is likewise responsible to some extent for the existing evils. The partial and defective enforcements of the laws are traceable in large measure to the character of the public official, and the character of the officials is dependent in

15 "Christianity and the Race Problem," p. 172.

turn upon the earnestness and honesty of the electorate. At times, in various sections of the South, one of the two candidates for office is a man who because of his past activities is renowned for fairness, a man who would undoubtedly try to afford the Negro whatever protection the Southern law guarantees. Yet the electorate in their selection of the candidate frequently ignore these qualifications. Thus they sin seriously against legal justice. The citizens in any democracy are morally bound, according to the teaching of the theologians, not only to vote but also to vote for the candidate who will promote the common good, who will concern himself about the welfare of all classes.[16] Moreover, according to the teaching of the theologians, restitution must be made at least by the railroad corporations and by the public officials. It should be made by the railroad corporations because an exorbitant fare has been collected from the Negroes. It should be made by the public officials because they are bound by a quasi-contract with the State to secure equal accommodations for the Negroes. Possibly this statement of the obligation of restitution is academic since the officials have no consciousness of committing a crime. But that unconsciousness of sin is not an indication of the venial character of the crime but rather of a calloused community conscience.

The ideal goal is of course the elimination of all racial barriers. Yet at the present time the only program of reform which could win the support of the Southern populace is one which strives to secure to the colored people equal but separate accommodations. That program must include emphasis from the pulpit on the immorality of the present practices and efforts by the Interracial Commission to remedy specific local abuses. The immediate possibilities of success are indicated in the statement of Woofter: "It has been the author's observation that the attitude of colored people toward separation in street cars in certain towns has been radically altered by the efforts of the company to secure uniform

16 Tanquerey, "Synopsis Theologiae Moralis," vol. III, n. 998.

courtesy and consideration on the part of the conductors."[17]

II. Segregation in Schools

In eighteen states black and white children are separated in the public schools by law. In four of these states the law even interdicts the teaching of both races in private schools. Florida debars a white person from acting as an instructor in a Negro school. A few of the states, however, requiring separation make an exception if the number eligible for school is small. Arizona requires eight for a separate school and Mississippi fifteen. In a few other states, such as Indiana, Wyoming, and Kansas, discretionary power relative to the erection of separate schools is given to the local school authorities.[18]

All such legislation was passed subsequent to the Civil War. Prior to that time the laws enacted by the Southern States were in complete restriction of any education or mental training of the Negro.[19] Even in some localities of the North an effort was also made by the populace to prevent the Negro from attending school. It is interesting to note, too, that as early as 1849, separate schools were provided by various Northern municipalities. During that year suit was brought against the City of Boston because such a policy had been inaugurated there and the Supreme Court of Massachusetts in decision on the case held the practice to be legal.[20] That policy was later abandoned by most of the Northern communities. But after the withdrawal of the Union forces the practice was adopted by the South and since then the constant trend of statutory law has been toward a complete separation. Moreover, those statutes as long as they did not conflict with the various State constitutions have been consistently regarded as valid by the United States Supreme Court. Indeed in

---

17 Op. cit., p. 239.
18 "Negro Year Book," p. 234.
19 Stroud, "Sketches of Laws Relating to Slavery," 1856.
20 *Illinois Law Review*, vol. XXI, p. 705, March, 1927.

the cases involving separation on common carriers the segregation of the race in the schools of Washington was averted to by the Court as a legal and reasonable arrangement.

The legislature which separates the races in Southern schools does not present a specifically new moral problem. The many gross wrongs which the Negro suffers because of inequitable enforcement have been treated in the fourth chapter. The principles, which were discussed above relative to the power of the States to separate the races on trains, seem to be applicable in this instance. Practically the same forces which necessitate separation in common carriers operate in this case. Truly the aversion of the white children toward the colored children is considerably less than that of white adults; and the compulsory attendance of both races at the same school would constitute a most forceful object lesson for the children in tolerance and in the brotherhood of man. Yet the fierce prejudice of the parents in the South at the present time renders such a policy impractical. Moreover, if equal school facilities were given to both races in the South separation would give immediate advantages to the Negro group. Positions are opened to colored teachers and colored superintendents who otherwise because of the prejudice would experience considerable difficulty in finding employment in those occupations.

The Northern cities which have received a large proportion of Negro migrants present a different moral problem. Though the laws of many of those States do not permit separation on the basis of color some white parents strive to effect the elimination of the Negro by pressure brought upon the school authorities. So at times segregation is virtually established.

As a justification for such practices various reasons are advanced by the parents and at times by the school authorities intimidated by the political influence of the parents. It is held that the colored children being mentally inferior retard the progress of the entire class. As observed above, the alleged mental inferiority of the colored group is still a mooted question. Anthropologists and other scholars who have received a scientific training challenge the contentions of those modern psychologists upon whose studies the assumption rests. Moreover, these psychologists themselves admit the existence of considerable overlapping between the races. So the proponents of the objection, if they profess to be scientific, must concede that only the colored children who have been proved inferior should be separated. That information could be obtained practically since mental measurements are used so widely in American educational institutions. But to attribute lower intelligence to a colored child simply because of his color is a defective process of reasoning. It is interesting to note that the Chicago Commission has declared: "The teachers who considered both races were inclined to believe that Negro children as a group had no special weaknesses that white children as a group did not also exhibit: that some children like any other children were good, some were bad and indifferent." "Many teachers asserted that the progress of Northern born Negro children compared very favorably with that of the whites."[21]

It has been objected that the presence of colored children introduces into the classroom antagonisms and dissensions which are inimical to study. But in the elementary schools of Chicago few disturbances, according to impartial studies, occurred in the classroom. "Most teachers agreed that there was little friction so far as school work was concerned."[22] At graduation some white parents protested against their children walking in the procession with the colored children but they confessed that only concern for the opinion of their neighbors motivated their action. In the high schools greater friction occurred. But it was manifested not in academic work but in the extra-curriculum activities such as glee clubs and social functions and never passed

21 "The Negro in Chicago," pp. 239-241.
22 Idem, p. 245.

beyond control. As to the conditions in other Northern cities an absolute statement is not possible. It appears to be a fair generalization that when serious friction has arisen it has been due to the supine policy of the local school board.

Another objection made by white parents to mixed schools is that such contacts lead to intermarriage. For the proper valuation of that objection it is helpful to recall several assumptions as regards the future which enjoys general acceptance. In the first place racial prejudice, though it is deplorable, and though serious efforts are being made to remove it, will undoubtedly continue for generations. Dr. Miller has observed: "The continuance of this intolerant spirit on the part of the white race in America is as certain as any other social tendency concerning which we now have predictive data."[23] Secondly, public sentiment against social intermingling will continue even longer. Thirdly, as the children grow into adolescence they will continue to be strongly influenced by the social practices of their parents. If proper allowance be made for those forces it must be admitted that there is very little connection between attendance at a grade school and intermarriage. The high schools present some difficulty because if the race mingled at parties and dances and if they visited one anothers' homes intermarriage might follow. But social intermingling is not necessary. The Chicago Commission reports: "In the purely social activities such as clubs and dances which are part of high school life there is none of the general mingling often found in semi-social activities such as singing and library societies."[24] In other words, contacts in public schools do not lead necessarily to the more intimate social commingling. Separation in social activities can be secured and regulated by the parents. The arrangement is not ideal but it secures to the Negro every educational op-

---

23 *South Atlantic Quarterly*, p. 242, July, 1926.
24 Op. cit., p. 235.

portunity and considering the gravity of the racial problem it seems to be a satisfactory adjustment.

A few parents claim that their children are exposed to moral dangers. Yet as it was observed in an earlier chapter every Negro child is not immoral. The moral weaknesses of the children which might be current in school would be to a considerable extent within the control of the authorities. It may be assumed that the white children have been blessed with some character.

The protest has also been raised that the white child suffers considerable inconvenience when he is compelled to attend a school which is frequented by Negro pupils. Yet it is a fact of common observation that a child is less conscious of racial differences and consequently he feels less repugnance. Furthermore, even in the most extreme practical case the Negroes would seldom constitute more than forty per cent of the enrollment. If their proportion tended to become greater the entire student body would probably become entirely Negroid for the whites quickly evacuate a district which has become dominantly colored. In the extreme practical case the inconvenience would not reach such magnitude as to justify separation. That statement cannot be proved, obviously. Yet it seems to be sufficiently probable to warrant provisional acceptance.

With the exception of the contention based upon the intelligence of the Negro the objections are not convincing. Frequently they are advanced by parents merely as a pretext or as a justification for an attitude motivated by convictions which they would hesitate to defend openly. They object to the presence of the Negro because of their sense of superiority, because they regard the Negro race as a lower order in the hierarchy of beings, because they feel that their prestige and position are compromised by contact with the colored upon a basis of equality.

The Negro in most Northern communities enjoys by law the right of attending the school proximate to his home and under normal conditions there is no compelling reason why that right should be denied him. Segregation is an abnormal condition, a scaffolding which enables the races to live together in a difficult situation, a practice which carries a strong presumption of giving the Negro inferior equipment and treatment, a condition which should be abolished as soon as it may be done prudently. Moreover, much good can come from limited contacts in schools. Through such contacts the white children acquire a deeper knowledge of the Negro, of his similar nature, of his ability, of his power of self-control. By contacts in schools current assumptions about the Negro are often dispelled. Such knowledge could lead in the future to more amicable race relations and dissolve for the coming generations in the North the intolerant prejudice which frequently closes the door of progress in industry and business to the colored man or woman.

The white parents who attempt to drive the colored child from the school attended by their offspring sin frequently against justice and charity. Against justice both because the Negro child enjoys from Northern States the right of attending the school proximate to his home and because the exclusion of the colored children is often secured by attacks on their persons and by defamation. Against charity because their actions are usually motivated by racial hatred and contempt and because they help to perpetuate prejudice.

III. Residential Segregation

Probably the phase of the Negro problem in which the largest number of people are vitally interested is residential segregation. The problem vexes both the North and the South. For the Northern cities already perplexed with a complicated housing problem have received during the last decade thousands of Negro migrants from the South. Following the practice of the South an attempt was made to force those migrants into those sections of the cities where the Negroes had always dwelt. But for numerous reasons both the colored migrant and his urban cousin refused to be thus restricted in their residence and insisted upon moving into sections occupied by whites. As a consequence, there has been engendered between the two races a wide-spread hostility. But before attempting a discussion of the morality of that form of segregation or of the actions of the people who have co-operated in the segregation, it may be profitable to examine some of the forces which have occasioned the present conflict.

The Social Forces

The obvious factor in the problem is, of course, the unwillingness of many white families to live in the same house or on the same street with Negroes; and the primary source of that unwillingness is prejudice. Prejudice, as it was stated in the third chapter, involves numerous elements which affect people differently. In respect to housing the social and conventional factors are especially vigorous. In many Southern cities Negroes live undisturbed in the alleys proximate to the white homes; and in border cities such as Washington the most exclusive apartment houses are sometimes built on streets on which the Negroes have dwelt for generations.[25] Though the social and conventional factors are important it would appear that aversion becomes the dominant factor if the influx of Negroes into a residential section places them in the majority. Furthermore, under such a condition another force is added to the aversion of the whites, the desire of the members of any national or social group to live among themselves. Since home connotes union with one's own and freedom from strangers many people, while indifferent to other contacts, are strongly opposed to dwelling within a group which differs strikingly from themselves. Various national groups freely gravitate toward specific centers in the large cities. Likewise, white people frequently object to the presence of Negroes in their residential districts.

---

25 *Christian Work*, vol. 119, p. 481.

The Physical Deterioration.

However, neither physical discomfort nor social prejudice but the fear of property depreciation explains the fierceness of the objection to the entrance of one colored family into a white district. From superficial observations made in colored sections of the city white people often assume that all Negroes are dirty, noisy, and destructive of property. They are apprehensive less such traits be introduced into their neighborhood. They fear as a consequence of the entrance of one colored family the loss of property value and the transformation of their section into a colored neighborhood. They have noted that if one colored family moves in all the white families move away; and they have been told that most of the property is sold at a considerable loss. So to preserve a desirable residential section and to protect a financial investment the entrance of even one colored family is passionately opposed.

But in the attitude assumed by the whites there are involved several false assumptions. All Negroes are not noisy; rather among them is an ever-increasing group which is quiet and refined. Secondly, the property deterioration and depreciation commonly regarded as a consequence of his presence is not entirely attributable to the presence of the Negro. Cities which know no Negro problem have their fluctuations in values and their delapidated districts.

Frequently the property which the Negroes rent or purchase in the Northern cities had already deteriorated before their entrance. Their dwellings are often old and bear palpable evidence of having been used by several European groups. For some years before the occupation of the property by the Negroes the owners had deliberately permitted it to deteriorate because it had bordered upon the black section. After the entrance of the Negroes the owners continued to neglect the property, partly because they hoped to capitalize the Negro's need and partly because they thought that the property would soon be transferred to industrial and commercial uses.

For it is a common observation that industry and commerce frequently follow closely upon the residence of the Negro. The Chicago Racial Commission has thus generalized upon conditions in that city: "There are many landlords who exact high rental from Negroes for the use of run-down houses. All investigations of Negro housing on the South Side indicated that as a rule the rents were excessive considering the inferior dwellings, their disrepair, and the unsanitary conditions. The neglect by the landlords not only directly depreciates the property but encourages a careless use of it by tenants."[26] In the South somewhat different conditions prevail. Yet a Southern woman, a student of social conditions, writes: "Many of the owners of property occupied by the colored make no effort to keep it in repair. Yet they collect from such property an annual profit of thirty per cent."[27]

A popular rejoinder to the statements made above is that even under Negro ownership the property continues to deteriorate. That statement may be an expression of a fact in many Northern cities. From that fact, however, the deduction need not be made, as it commonly is done, that the colored as a group are extremely careless and abuse property. Frequently the Negroes, because of the shortage of housing, are forced to pay such a high price for the property that they are unable to make the repairs. To quote from the report of the Chicago Commission again: "Many Negroes purchase fairly substantial dwellings on the long time instalment plan without providing for repairs and maintenance. Usually the monthly payment to cover interest, taxes and instalment on principle was about all the Negro and his family could carry even though his wife's wages supplemented his own."[28] In the North boarders and lodgers are taken in by a family in order to help with the payment. Such a condition accelerates the deterioration.

26 "The Negro in Chicago," p. 203.
27 "The Negro Women of Gainesville, Georgia," p. 20.
28 Op. cit., p. 200.

In the study of the Negro women of Gainesville, Ga., the author found that the ownership of a house greatly affected its condition. Of the houses owned by Negroes, 39 per cent were found to be in good condition, 45 per cent in fair condition, and 16 per cent in bad condition; while of those rented, 23 per cent were in good condition, 36 per cent in fair condition, and 41 per cent in bad condition.

Such statements do not exonerate the Negroes from all responsibility for the spectacular deterioration. It is a common opinion among real estate men that Negroes treat property more roughly than a corresponding class of whites. Yet those statements indicate the possibility of a partial vindication and they furnish a strong presumption that a cultured class would for most purposes use property as carefully as white people.

The Depreciation in Value.

As regards the depreciation in value, it is possibly true as a general statement that the market value of property drops slightly when a Negro family has moved into a district. But the Mayor's Race Committee in Detroit reports: "Our survey shows conclusively that in many instances where the colored population filtered into white residential sections making them ultimately colored sections there was no loss of real estate value and in many cases the rental and sale price increased. We believe that frequently where property depreciation does occur, it is due to the expectation that it will occur: that is, the hysteria in the neighborhood in which the penetration has begun causes many homes to be thrown upon the market and depreciation becomes inevitable."[29] The presence of one colored family does not constitute an objective justification for a marked drop in values. The district still remains desirable for white residential purposes. Actually, however, the owners become frequently panic-stricken and grow distrustful of one another.

29 Publications of the Detroit Bureau of Research, n. 108, p. 4.

Fearing that a neighbor might sell they all place their property on the market simultaneously and sell at a sacrifice. The City of Chicago furnishes several instances not only of persistence but even of increase in value in contested sections when the majority of the whites determined to remain or waited for a fair sale.[30] In those districts of Washington which have lately been hurriedly evacuated, few white families, according to the statements of competent real estate brokers, sold at a considerable loss. It seems that the whites themselves are largely responsible for the decline in values. In fact they are rather the cause and the Negro is only the occasion.

Neither in a discussion of the decline of property values should the activities of a certain class of white real estate agents be overlooked. To sell newly constructed, suburban homes, those agents occasionally make an extremely high allowance to a white family for their home in a white neighborhood and the house is accepted in partial payment. The reason for the high allowance is a prospective sale of the property to a Negro who because of the congestion in the colored district is willing to pay an exorbitant price for a home in a respectable neighborhood. The hope is also entertained by these agents that after the entrance of the colored family the other white people may be induced to follow their former neighbor to the newly-developed suburbs. As the Chicago Commission observed: "That depreciation of property generally charged exclusively to the presence of Negroes in a neighborhood is often largely due to other factors." [31]

The Existing Colored Districts.

Another condition which has contributed greatly to the present strained situation is the dire shortage of adequate housing accommodations for colored families. An occasional Negro may move into a white neighborhood

---

30 "The Negro in Chicago," p. 212.
31 Idem, p. 646.

solely for the purpose of having contact with whites or to exercise his independence. But the overwhelming majority of colored people being very human prefer to dwell among their own. They enter white sections only because of the absence of adequate and desirable housing accommodations in the Negro sections.

In 1913, a writer in the Annals of the American Academy of Political and Social Science declared that the colored sections of Northern cities were very congested and that very meager accommodations were offered for the more cultured group.[32] Since then the Negro population of those cities has been doubled by migration from the South. In the absence of new construction some of the Negroes were forced to seek accommodations among the whites. But it was not the migrant but rather the Northern Negro who moved into the white sections. Since their standards of living had been raised by popular education they had become conscious of the disreputable and squalid conditions prevalent in the black belt, and they had felt impelled to seek relief. For the streets in the colored section are usually neglected by the municipal officials and the houses, being old, are devoid of many facilities. "The ordinary conveniences considered necessities by the average white citizen are lacking. Bathrooms are often missing, heating is commonly done in coal stoves, and furnaces are rather exceptional."[33] An investigator of the conditions of the colored migrants in Philadelphia writes that their houses were with few exceptions in an exceedingly poor physical condition.[34] In Cincinnati a survey indicated that fifty-four per cent of the Negro homes were without baths.[35] Furthermore, not only unsanitary but even immoral conditions are rampant in the colored section because they lack police influence. In 1919 the Chicago Commission found: "The border land of a colored residential district is the haven

32 *Annals of American Academy*, vol. 48, p. 108.
33 "The Negro in Chicago," p. 205.
34 *Annals of American Academy*, vol. 98, p. 208.
35 *Proceedings of N. C. S. W.*, vol. 524, 1919

for disorderly resorts. Protests of colored residents against the painted women in their neighborhood and the loud profanity and vulgarity are usually ignored by the police.[36]

The question is occasionally asked why do not the Negroes develop new tracts of land in the suburbs instead of entering white sections. For their inactivity along those lines there is a very plausible explanation. Frequently the most desirable and easily developed suburban districts have already fallen into the control of white people. To develop the remaining sections considerable capital would be necessary and so they are closed to the Negro. Although a few colored individuals may own considerable wealth the Negroes as a group have not acquired sufficient financial resources of their own to undertake such extensive operations. Neither may they borrow the money since the color line extends even into the bank. The observation made in Chicago is generally true of every Northern city: "Most real estate firms and loan companies decline to make loans on property owned or occupied by Negroes."[37] The Detroit Committee similarly observed that, "In order to make the acquisition and maintenance of good standards of Negro housing possible it is necessary for banking and loaning institutions to be more liberal in their attitude toward Negro loans."[38] One Northern philanthropist who was contemplating the development of a suburb for the colored was forced to abandon his project because of opposition. He was told: "You will ruin the street-car line."[39]

It may be further objected that there are already in existence several Negro suburbs which are not patronized. The proponents of such an objection have probably never closely examined the colored suburbs. Usually they are colored suburbs because the physical con-

36 Op. cit., p. 202.
37 "The Negro in Chicago," p. 221.
38 *Detroit Bureau of Governmental Research*, n. 108, p. 5.
39 "The Negro in Chicago," p. 225.

ditions would repel the poorest white class. In 1919, Chicago had several subdivisions such as Lillydale but they were glaring examples of exploitation. At that time Lillydale was without paving, lighting and sidewalks; and Robbins, a Negro village outside of the city, was physically unattractive and a long mile from the car line.[40] The Negro subdivision in Washington is handicapped by the absence of sidewalks and a poor quality of buildings. The Detroit Committee, in describing the subdivision of that city, said: "It was unsanitary beyond redemption."

The protest may be made finally that the Negroes could do much to improve the districts in which they now reside. Undoubtedly the districts would be improved if the leaders of the colored group thought less of moving elsewhere. But that is only a partial remedy. Many dwellings are beyond repair and their present districts are inadequate in extent. So until some serious effort is made by the different communities to remedy present conditions the colored families desirous of dwelling in pleasant and attractive homes must continue to seek houses in white districts.

The Moral Implications

In discussing the morality of other forms of segregation attention was given to the laws of Southern States by which the races are separated. Residential segregation, however, offers no occasion for discussing the justice of either the state laws or the municipal ordinances which would separate the races into residential districts. Although several Southern cities are still attempting to enforce such legislation the ordinances are unquestionably illegal. In November, 1917, the Supreme Court of the United States rendered a decision which virtually declared all ordinances of that character to be unconstitutional. The occasion of the decision was the Buchanan v. Warley case in which an ordinance of the City of Louis-

---

40 Op. cit., p. 139 and p. 225.

ville, Kentucky, restricting the residence of both races to specific sections was contested. The Court declared that the ordinance which bases the interdiction upon color and nothing more passes beyond the legitimate bounds of the police power and invades the civil right to acquire and to use property, a right which is enjoyed by all citizens.[41] In 1927, a case against the City of New Orleans was decided similarly without comment. The average layman may find it difficult to understand why the State may segregate the races in schools and in common carriers but not in regard to residential sections. The decision has been designated by one legal periodical as an example of the "peculiar solicitude of American courts for property rights." But at any rate the laws are illegal and presumably unjust; and the segregation of the Negro has been left to the initiative of white individuals.

Such a condition makes a moral discussion of the subject extremely difficult both because of the meager co-operation of each individual and because in such matters as the selling and the renting of houses considerable freedom is permitted by the theologians. Father Kelleher has observed, "Mere discrimination in social or business matters, however much it may savor of bigotry or narrow-mindedness in certain circumstances cannot be called immoral." [42]

However, there can be no question about the morality of some practices resorted to by white people at the present time to discourage Negroes from entering their districts. Bombing, the defacement of property, insults, intimidation by mass gatherings, and other acts of violence are grave injustices and the co-operators therein are bound to restitution. When a colored family has legally purchased a home they acquire all the rights thereto enjoyed by white people in similar circumstances. To them must be rendered the accepted marks of respect and con-

---

41 U. S. Reports, vol. 245, p. 61, Oct. Term, 1917.
42 Catholic Encyclopedia, Index vol., p. 13.

sideration shown to other neighbors. The denial of such courtesies is frequently equivalent to a manifestation of hatred.

The White Property Owner.

If the Negro is merely seeking the purchase of a home the white man who has placed his property on the market is evidently not bound in justice to sell. Is he bound to refuse a sale to the Negro? Some people believe that because of charity for his white neighbors he should not transfer his property to a colored man as long as he can find a white purchaser. In view of the conditions prevalent in most American cities it seems that rather the Negro should be the object of charity. The financial loss to the neighbors directly consequent from such a sale is not great. If later, because of the entrance of many colored people, the district ceases to be a desirable place for residences there are other pleasant districts where the white families may easily settle. Their inconvenience is material. On the other hand the inconvenience suffered by the Negro under such circumstances is of a higher order. The purchase or the rental of such property by the Negro probably means relief from squalid conditions which are seriously inimical to the physical and moral well-being of his family. His need of proper housing accommodations is in a certain sense a spiritual need. Consequently it seems that in charity the Negro is entitled to consideration. The white neighbors in their objection to the entrance of a few Negro families are forgetful of the grave Christian duty incumbent upon them of assisting the weak to obtain proper housing accommodations. A writer of a pamphlet on rural housing published by the English Catholic Truth Society states: "If it be found that in this country that the homes of large numbers of the rural labouring population are such as tend to degrade them physically and morally then all good Catholics are bound by the duty of charity even at the cost of considerable self-sacrifice to take every means, political, social, and personal of removing the causes of such grave scandal to their fellow Christians."[43] The same statement is applicable to the obligations of white people toward the Negroes. Since the present housing accommodations for the colored are inadequate it seems that the general duty of exercising charity toward white neighbors does not forbid a white owner to transfer his property to a Negro.

If the Negro were confronted only with the scruples of individual whites about acting uncharitably toward their neighbors his housing problem would be simple. But frequently he finds himself facing a more serious situation; he finds that many of the inhabitants of a district have agreed and conspired among themselves to sell only to whites. Such agreements are regarded by the colored as serious injustices.

What is the moral character of such an agreement? It is true that conspiracy or agreement constitutes a new and essential note which sharply distinguishes the group action from the action of the individual. The action of such a group assumes a character analogous to those actions which people designate as strikes and boycotts. Like a strike or a boycott it is not always immoral. But it may become immoral because of the end or because of the means used.[44] As regards the end it appears that an agreement or conspiracy made for the purpose of excluding a few Negro families from entering a white section is uncharitable. The Negro's need is greater than the inconvenience suffered by the white residents. However, opposition to the entrance of a large number of colored families would not constitute an offense against charity. For if each section received without protest a few Negro families the Negro's need would be substantially relieved. Neither is such an agreement necessarily unjust. The Negro has no strict right to the rental or the purchase of any particular house. However, the Negro does enjoy the right to be free from illicit inter-

---

43 Toke, "Rural Housing," p. 3.

44 Noldin, op. cit., vol. II, p. 323.

ference when he is seeking the purchase or the rental of any property. At the present time many of the actions of such organizations of property owners seem to contravene the freedom of the Negro and are consequently unjust.

A group of citizens might, without violating the rights of the Negro, exhort other neighbors privately not to sell. Public meetings held for that purpose are condemnable because of the almost inseparable abuses involved. The speeches are invariably inflammatory. In such assemblies the Negroes as a group are abused, maligned, and defamed. Ignorance, fear, prejudice, and the protective impulses of white men are played upon. In the past such meetings have frequently awakened dormant antipathies and precipitated serious crises.

Restrictive Covenants.

Besides mass meetings, another method which is being used widely is the drafting and the signing of a covenant binding a certain group of property owners not to sell for a certain period of years to a Negro. Such covenants have been recognized as valid by courts in Michigan and California. More recently the Court of Appeals of the District of Columbia has approved the decision of a court of equity which granted an injunction restraining a participant in such a covenant from conveying his property to a Negro.[45] A few other courts throughout the country, however, have declared such covenants unconstitutional but such decisions are exceptional. A writer in the Illinois Law Review has stated: "These cases are growing in number and an examination of them and of the general trend of judicial opinion leads one to believe that private racial zoning contracts as to use but not to conveyance or alienation and which are limited to a reasonable time and to limited persons or limited classes of persons, such as the Negroes or the Chinese, will be sustained by the courts."[46]

---

45 Corrigan v. Buckley, Federal Reporter, v. 229, p. 899.
46 *Illinois Law Review,* Vo. 121, n. 7, March, 1927, p. 713.

These decisions of the courts are very regrettable and savor of injustice because they constitute at the present time a serious handicap for the Negro in his search for a respectable home. As the Court of the District of Columbia observed, such covenants in themselves violate no constitutional prerogative. The Negro's constitutional right to acquire property does not carry with it the power to compel the sale of any particular property. The protective clauses of the Fifth and the Fourteenth Amendments are inhibitions upon the power of the general government and of the states respectfully and not upon the actions of individuals. The fundamental question involved was whether the covenants were of such a discriminatory character as to be unenforceable by a court of equity. The Court held that they were not of such a character since the ordinances of various States requiring separation in trains and schools had been regarded as legal and reasonable.

In that statement it appears that the Court failed to give sufficient advertence to the essential difference existing between the segregation effected by ordinance and the segregation effected by their decision. Any segregation ordinance enjoys validity only to the extent that it guarantees equal accommodations to both races and that the executive offices are empowered to procure its equitable enforcement. The effect of the decision of the Court is different. It assists the white residents in the exclusion of the black man from desirable property now occupied by the whites. But no provision is made for securing to the Negro equal accommodations. The decision might possibly be used under certain circumstances to crystallize the present inequitable division of accommodations. Segregation by ordinance guarantees to the colored equal accommodations while segregation by courts of equity does not.

The Courts, to confirm their statement that covenants were not discriminatory but rather equitable, stated:

"The power of these property owners to exclude one class of citizens implies the power of the other class to exercise the same prerogatives on property they may own." Again the Court failed to make sufficient allowance for the difference between legal and actual equality. Though the races may be equal before the law, in actual life they are very unequal. The white race in this matter possess great power and the black race very little. Furthermore, as a consequence of the decision, a condition might possibly be created that would render it impossible for the Negro to exercise at any time any control over residential sites.

The decisions then are inequitable. By emphasizing a purely theoretical equality before the law they actually place the weaker group at the mercy of the stronger group. They allow, not a government pledged to justice, but a group of white individuals to regulate the housing accommodations of the Negroes. Furthermore, the enforcement of the covenant by a court of equity under present conditions violates a natural right of the Negro. The right violated is that of being free from illicit interference when seeking the purchase or rental of a house. The illicit interference is unreasonable force. For the use of force by government becomes unreasonable when it is used contrary to the end of a government; when it is used to protect the interests of its stronger citizens without making provision for the interests of its weaker citizens. However, the decisions of those Courts are not final. There is a possibility that the Supreme Court of the United States may, in the future, reverse those decisions. Because the Corrigan v. Buckley case was dismissed for want of jurisdiction and the court did not examine the merits of the contention that the indenture was "of such a discriminatory nature that a court of equity should not lend its aid by enforcing its performance."[47]

---

47 Supreme Court, No. 104, Oct. Term, 1925; decision rendered May 24, 1926.

It must be recognized that the Negro is not excluded by these covenants from all property now controlled by whites. Houses in the new developments are practically closed to him because of the restrictions attached to the deeds by the original developers. In the districts far removed from the black belt many owners, feeling secure, do not wish to pay an attorney's fee for the drawing up of a legal covenant. In adjoining districts some owners refuse to sign, believing that because of conditions peculiar to their property they could sell to the Negro with greater profit. Another group refuse to sign because of conscientious reasons. Yet, if a concerted effort were made to induce more people to enter such agreements the Negro could be effectually excluded.

Are property owners acting righteously in signing those covenants? At present, when housing accommodations are so inadequate the signers usually sin against charity. A confirmation of that opinion is the fact that there are a number of conscientious people who hesitate to sign. But the covenant itself becomes clearly unjust only when enforced by the court. The signing under protest is rather remote co-operation and it might be permitted for a serious reason.

Real Estate Associations.

Besides the property owners, local associations of real estate men have contributed toward the exclusion of the Negro. These associations concern themselves very much with the debarment of Negroes from white sections and interest themselves very little in securing adequate housing for the colored group elsewhere. Usually the members are pledged not to sell property in a white district to a Negro. Obviously, because of the power enjoyed by such an association the Negro suffers greatly. The majority of the prominent real estate agents are usually members of the directing board of such an association. Thus the Negro's entrance into many of the older districts is within control of the association. Furthermore, the undeveloped suburban districts are closed by them to the Negro. Banks, loaning houses, municipal officials, park boards, transit companies, and other agencies which co-operate in the development of a new district are also influenced by the actions of real estate organizations. The development of entire sections of a city are at times within their control. Their national association has thus defined a realtor: "I am an idealist striving ever to better civic conditions and laboring for the happiness and the prosperity of my fellowman; I tap the resources of a nation, develop tractless wastes into thriving, hustling, happy communities, and of my enthusiasm and energy, great cities are born."[48]

In view of the scarcity of respectable colored residential districts the actions of these associations seem to constitute an injustice. The right of the colored man which is violated is his right to seek or pursue a lawful good without hindrance through unjust means.[49] The unjust means in this case is the abuse of office. Because of their position those real estate associations have a social responsibility. They are something more than private societies. To them is entrusted at present the distribution of housing accommodations. Because of that position they are bound by distributive justice to apportion equitably those accommodations. Their social obligation in the matter of housing is analogous to the obligation of the employer in the matter of wages. They abuse their office when, without making any adequate provision or allowance for the needs of the Negro they agree not to sell property to a Negro in existing white neighborhoods. By the false use of their office they prevent the Negro from seeking a legitimate good and commit an injustice. The responsibility for the injustice falls principally upon the influential members who dominate the policies.

If, on the other hand, the Negro population were adequately housed and if the association were earnestly en-

---

48 *Washington Post,* Feb. 20, 1927.
49 Lehmkuhl, op. cit., n. 1161.

deavoring to secure new and desirable districts for them then an agreement not to sell houses in a white section to the colored might be equitable if such an agreement were necessary to stabilize values. Under such circumstances their action could scarcely be considered as an abuse of office.

Remedies.

The remedies for such a complex situation must be numerous. Many activities, if undertaken by individuals or groups in the community would alleviate somewhat the present strained conditions. Wider publicity should be given to truths which are unknown to many white citizens. The people should be reminded of the existence of a cultured and refined group among the Negroes. They should be informed that the depreciation of property values is often due to factors other than the presence of the colored. Municipal officials should concern themselves more about the paving, the lighting, and the sanitation of colored districts. Wealthy philanthropists could profitably imitate the example of Mr. Rockefeller, who recently built several apartment houses for the colored in Harlem.[50] But since the problem is dominantly social it must be met not only by the actions of individuals but especially by some specific social organization similar to the Interracial Commission of the South. As yet, no standard organization in Northern cities has been devised. But such a commission could easily be formed and should be composed of municipal officials, representatives of the real estate boards and the Negro leaders. Possibly it might be made an integral part of the planning commissions for urban growth which are being organized in the larger cities. The decisions of such a Commission would lack official enforcement but because of the wide social influence they could accomplish much. The possibilities are suggested in the news item that in Louisville, Kentucky: "A whole section of the city to which Negroes had been denied access was turned over

50 *Opportunity*, Jan., 1927, p. 14.

completely to Negro occupancy after a conference with real estate organizations, the Woman's City Club, and the city authorities."[51]

The obligation for the formation of such a commission rests primarily upon the public officials and the real estate associations. A correlative obligation of supporting it rests also upon the citizen. But the success of their effort will depend entirely upon their seriousness in making equitable apportionments. The concession must be real and adequate. It will involve sacrifices from the whites in the surrender of attractive residential sections and sacrifices from the real estate dealers in the forfeiture of exhorbitant profits. But if the division is prudently made no person should lose.[52]

The Negro must, in turn, agree to confine for some years his residence to the district agreed upon. Such agreement will involve restraint upon freedom. Yet it seems necessary because of the existence of such a virulent prejudice which neither good-will nor law can immediately efface. Before abnormal situations men have always been asked to make concessions. If the Negro leaders should refuse to co-operate in such an understanding and insist upon the exercise of their freedom they will assume a most imprudent course. The more powerful will undoubtedly succeed in entering white neighborhoods but the poorer Negroes will bear the burden. Prejudices will be accentuated and influential white people who have struggled to obtain recognition of the more fundamental rights of the colored man may be alienated.

---

51 *Opportunity,* Jan., 1927, p. 14.
52 Cf. *Current History,* March, 1927, p. 83.

CHAPTER VII

ECONOMIC DISCRIMINATIONS

The right to obtain from one's present occupation the means of a decent livelihood and the right in the pursuit of employment in more lucrative occupations to be free from unreasonable interference are prerogatives especially precious to all men. Man's well-being, progress, and contentment depend upon them in a large measure. The Negro, in the exercise of these rights, feels that he is seriously handicapped and restricted because of his color. He believes that the poverty which characterizes his race is due in large measure to the violation of his rights. Such great importance is attributed to these discriminations that Dr. Moton of Tuskegee has written: "It is not too much to say that if the Negro could in every case receive economic justice a large part of what we call the race problem would be solved. In many cases he would be in position to solve his own problems."[1] Consequently, in the subsequent paragraphs, an attempt will be made to examine some of the contacts which the Negro in the pursuit of his livelihood has made in the fields of agriculture, industry and commerce, and to discuss a few of the discriminations to which he is subject. For convenience, the discussion will be grouped under the titles: "The Negro on the Farm" and "The Negro in the City."

THE NEGRO ON THE FARM

The African slaves that were imported into this continent a little less than three centuries ago were used extensively as unskilled laborers on large farms and plantations. Today the livelihood of the American Negro is, to a large extent, bound up with agriculture.

---

1 "Cooperation in Soutnern Communities," p. 33.

Of the farmers in the United States, 14.3 per cent are Negroes. Of the Negro group itself, approximately 66 per cent are engaged in agricultural pursuits. They raise 37 per cent of the cotton crop, 20 per cent of the corn, 16 per cent of the potatoes, and 15 per cent of the hay and forage.[2] These conditions prevail despite the spectacular migrations to the cities between 1910 and 1920, which took over 700,000 colored people from the farm and reduced the colored rural population by 3.3 per cent.

Prevailing Conditions

The condition of the Negro on the farm has its bright and dark facets. The bright picture is delineated in the progress which the race has made since emancipation. In 1865, the Negroes were to a considerable extent illiterate and owned very little property. Some were but a generation from savagery. Since then their development has been phenomenal. The value of the land and buildings owned by the Negro farmers of the South in 1920 was estimated at $522,178,137. Between 1900 and 1910, the value of land and buildings owned by Negroes increased 293 per cent, and with the exception of the decade between 1910 and 1920, the number of farm owners has increased constantly. The progress of some Negroes is graphically indicated in the account which the Negro Year Book gives of a colored farmer living near Lawrence, Kansas. This Negro made a specialty of truck gardening and from a 12-acre farm realized a profit of $6000 a year. His four sons and two daughters are graduates of the Kansas State University.[3]

But the darker side becomes evident from even a superficial glance at the condition of the masses of Negroes engaged in agriculture. Of the Negro farmers but 10.1 per cent are owners, while 32.4 per cent are tenants and 57.5 per cent are laborers. Of the tenants less

---

2 "The Negro Year Book," pp. 376-380.

3 Op. cit., p. 2.

than one-third are cash tenants while the remainder are share tenants. The proportion of the share tenants portends a grave situation. The share tenant is supplied with tools, machinery, seed, and other necessities as well as with land and farm equipment. When the crop is harvested, from the Negro's share is deducted a charge for the supplies furnished during the year, and in estimating the charge the owner always includes an insurance and interest item. Consequently, the tenant is frequently so deeply in debt that his share of the crop may be insufficient to cover his obligation. His plight, howover, does not necessarily imply dishonesty on the part of the land owner, since the Negro's ignorance and poverty are serious liabilities. Though the condition of the share tenant may be bad, that of the laborer is worse. Their wages, though the work is seasonal, range only from $1 to $3 a day.[4]

The living conditions of practically all classes of Negroes engaged in agriculture are deplorable. Food is very expensive, for the merchant, in determining the price, must make allowance for heavy transportation charges and also for interest. All supplies are bought on credit. Their homes are generally intolerably bad and lacking in the most elementary conveniences. The work, because of the system of farming, is monotonous and uninteresting. In no way does the Negro farmer's life compare with the picture which the New Englander or the Westerner entertains of a farmer. For gardens, cows and hogs are rare, and there are "thousands of tenant farms without a chicken."[5]

The point which is deserving of special emphasis is that many of those evils which afflict the Negro farmers are due not to discrimination but to a most unfortunate system of agriculture which has been saddled upon the South. The condition of the white farmer is almost as intolerable. Dr. Woofter has observed of the white farmer: "In long periods of low and medium prices the

---

4 "Negro Year Book," p. 6.
5 Woofter, "The Basis of Racial Adjustment," p. 80.

farmer has barely made interest on his invested capital and has often suffered disaster."[6] A large percentage of the white farm operators are only tenants who are migrating constantly, seeking better conditions. Between 1910 and 1920 almost two million Southern whites migrated from their native States.[7] Recent studies made by professors from the University of North Carolina have revealed a most desperate poverty among the white tenants of that State. In several counties of the State the income of the white farm laborer was found to be but a few cents greater than that of the Negro.[8]

Such conditions are explained in large part by the prevalence of the "single crop system" in the South. The Civil War left the South heavily in debt but possessing her traditional monopoly over the world's cotton market. Since then the Southern planter has borrowed heavily on the prospective crop and has attempted to increase profits by growing cotton exclusively and by continuing the pre-war practice of importing from other states foodstuffs and farm supplies. On those imported goods freight and a profit to the grower have been paid.[9] Yet the profits from the cotton crop have never been sufficient to cover those added expenses and at the same time to free the grower from the grasp of the loan capitalist. In order to remedy the situation the grower has frequently further immeshed himself by increasing his money acreage crop and by neglecting his subsidiary crops.[10] No monopolistic price has been realized because to pay his debts the grower was forced to sell the crop early. The practice has developed to such an extent that when the farmer attempts to market anything but cotton he finds it difficult to secure credit. Lately that serious situation has been aggravated by the ravages of the boll-weevil. Thus the "single crop system," as Tannenbaum observed, "develops tenancy, causes migra-

---

6 Idem, p. 75.
7 Dowd, "The Negro in American Life," p. 251.
8 Tannenbaum, "Darker Phases of the South," p. 133.
9 Cf. Helper, "The Impending Crisis."
10 Weatherford, "The Negro from Africa to America," p. 266.

tions, affects the literacy of the community, depletes the soil, places the producer at the mercy of the creditor, fosters political bossism, destroys the traditional stability of the farm."[11] The Negroes in company with many whites are the victims.

Unfair Practices

Current in the present system are certain unfair practices which accentuate the Negro's hardships and increase his burdens. One of the unfair practices has its origin in the laxity of the tenant agreements, especially those between the owners and the share tenants. In many instances there are no written contracts and strict accounts of the loans made to the Negroes are not kept. When settlement is made at the end of the year, "some of the landlords willfully take advantage of their tenant's ignorance and helplessness and appropriate his share of the crop as well as their own."[12] They farm the Negro rather than the land. Such a practice is the grossest form of robbery. The education of the Negro and the enactment of a law making contracts unenforceable unless written would undoubtedly correct much of the abuse.

A second unfair practice is the inequitable distribution of rural credits. Under such an agricultural system the opportunity of obtaining long-time credits is indispensable. The Federal Government in 1916 attempted to alleviate that need of the farmers in the South and the West by the institution of Federal Farm Banks through which the owners of farm lands might borrow money on terms convenient to themselves. But the assistance offered by the Federal Government, though a boon to the white farmer, has meant very little to the Negro. Loans are made not to individuals but to groups who apply through a local agent. In many localities the Negro has experienced the greatest difficulty in gaining admission to those groups.

---

11 Tannenbaum, op. cit., p. 144.
12 Woofter, op. cit., p. 88.

In localities where the thrifty Negroes are too few to organize, the action of the white group in refusing admittance to the Negro constitutes obviously a serious injustice. However, in many districts ignorance and lack of initiative on the part of the Negroes are partly responsible since the number of farm owners necessary to form such a group is only ten. The late Dr. Scaborough, a Negro associated with the Department of Agriculture as a specialist, was making, prior to his death, serious efforts to correct those abuses which he thought were due to the local farm groups and not to the Regional banks.[13]

A third unfair practice is the discrimination practiced in the appointment of farm demonstration agents. These agents, who are paid in part by the extension service of the United States Department of Agriculture, give to the farmers of a specific locality instruction in agriculture and domestic economy. The benefits which accrue to a Southern farmer from contact with one of those agents almost challenge exaggeration. Weatherford writes: "By means of these methods as well as by increase in acreage, the quality and value of farm crops almost doubled between 1910 and 1920."[14] Unfortunately, the colored group have not received their proportionate share of such training. Only a few of the agents are Negroes and the white agents, either because of prejudice or because of the great needs of the white farmers, seldom visit the colored farmers. Dr. Moton has written that of the 1700 agents employed by the Department of Agriculture but 240 were colored. The State of South Carolina, with 109,000 Negro farmers, has only one colored agent.[15]

The responsibility for that inequitable distribution rests primarily upon the county officials. For while the agents are under control of the Federal Department of Agriculture they are financed in part by the county and state funds and they are appointed at the request of the

---

13 *Opportunity,* Feb., 1926, p. 66.
14 Op. cit., p. 266.
15 "Cooperation in Southern Communities," p. 24.

local authorities. Such discrimination is clearly a grave injustice and the observations made about the culpability of public officials relative to the distribution of school funds are applicable in this instance.

The Negro in the City

Like the entire national population of which they are a component part the American Negroes have manifested a strong tendency to move into the city. Between 1910 and 1920 the colored urban group increased by 870,244.

In the city the occupations in which they are gainfully employed depend greatly upon the locality. In both Northern and Southern cities domestic service has yielded them employment more than any other occupation. According to the census of 1920, twenty-two per cent of the race were employed in domestic and personal service. A large proportion of that group were women. Lately, however, the members of the colored race have manifested a tendency to abandon that work. A partial explanation of that movement in the South may be found in the prevailing low standard of wages.[16] In the North a similar tendency prevails despite attractive remuneration. The more potent reason is the objection to the long hours and the isolation. It might be interesting to the white race to note that a protest has been raised by some of the religious colored leaders against the members of their race engaging in domestic service because of the moral dangers.[17]

The withdrawal of the colored group from domestic service has good and evil consequences. One very encouraging result is that some of the women, who have abandoned such service, are remaining at home rather than entering other occupations. On the other hand, as an effect of that movement racial prejudice, at least in the South, is being increased. Formerly only the best class of the Negro group were engaged in domestic service. Today the weaker members are thus employed and

---

16 Woofter, op. cit., p. 9.
17 Idem, p. 258.

since they alone are met by a large proportion of white individuals, judgment is passed upon the entire race from such contacts. The Southern housewives are aggravated by the nomadic traits of the women they employ as maids and cooks. The author of "The Negro Women of Gainsville, Ga." stated that only thirty per cent of the colored women engaged in domestic service in that town remained more than three months with one family. Some worked only until they had secured funds for a new dress and others would come in from the country and engage in service until they were again needed upon the farm. But it was also discovered that length of service was related to the amount paid in salary and that the white women occasioned some of the overturn by bidding for the service of colored girls already employed.[18]

Southern Industry and the Negro

The employment of the Negroes in other urban occupations varies widely with the section of the nation in which the Negro chances to reside. In the South, prior to the Civil War, textile mills, foundries, and other industries were rare. The section was dominantly agricultural and the only manual tasks beside farming at which a large number of men could be profitably employed were the skilled trades. Such work was performed at times by the Negroes. Judging from contemporary testimony it was done satisfactorily. The poor whites in the cities vigorously objected to the employment of Negroes, slave or free, in such skilled work. In 1831, the mechanics of Concord, North Carolina, for example, protested against the action of the slave-holders who used their slave mechanics and underbid them in contracts. It was alleged by the signers of the protest that the Negroes "took away business that belonged to white laborers."[19] Other groups in the various communities also protested that the training of the Negro as

---

18 Reed, "The Negro Women of Gainesville, Ga.," p. 26.
19 Wesley, "Negro Labor in the United States," p. 72.

an artisan and mechanic would unfit him for slavery. Despite such opposition the slave-owners, because of obvious economic advantages, remained obdurate.

After the Civil War a great social revolution broke out in the South. The poor whites rebelled against the control exercised by the former slave-owners over political and social life. The revolution, though less spectacular than the War for Southern Independence, affected drastically the life of the various classes of the Southern States.[20] Since it rose slowly like a giant from sleep and since it warred against practices which were imbedded in age-old customs the struggle is not completed and its effects are uncertain. One obvious result of that movement, however, has been the breaking of the Negro's control over the skilled trades. The poor whites competed against the Negroes in the skilled trades and when the competition grew keen they appealed to the entire white race for support on the basis of their color. Lately, even a larger number of whites have been drawn to the skilled trades by the increase in wages and the favorable working conditions which the trade unions have secured.

Though the Negro has lost control over those trades he is still able to find extensive employment, and there is even a faint indication that the pendulum may swing back. In a recent survey made by a member of the Tuskegee teaching staff it was found that 70 per cent of the carpenters, 80 per cent of the tailors, and 95 per cent of the shoe repairers who completed their respective trades at Tuskegee were actively employed at the trades for which thy had been trained.[21] So in the South, despite extensive discriminations, there are considerable opportunities open to the colored craftsman.

In the few mills and factories which were operated in the South prior to the Rebellion, Negroes were occasionally employed and proved themselves efficient fac-

---

20 Murphy, "The Basis of Ascendancy," p. 12.
21 *Opportunity*, Feb., 1926, p. 59.

tory hands. In fact, their success was such that Southern statesmen dreamt of securing a monopoly over the nation's industries by the use of cheap slave labor. Efforts were even made to interest the planters in such projects.[22] But most of the employes in the mills before the Civil War were whites. As the industry developed after the War those trained workers opposed the introduction of the Negroes, and since at that time there was an abundance of white labor that field of activity was gradually closed. Recently there has been some increase in the number of Negroes engaged in textile mills. Yet the increase has not been in proportion to the expansion of that industry.[23] Other occupations, such as cab driving, are open to the Negroes in some cities but the color line is drawn very arbitrarily.

Northern Industry and the Negro

The Negro in the North, prior to the World War, experienced much greater difficulty in securing employment than in the South. In the early part of the nineteenth century the free Negroes who resided in the North were, with few exceptions, domestics and unskilled laborers. But as the century advanced the colored man was forced from many of those occupations by the thousands of Irish and German immigrants who came into the country. During the Civil War an attempt was made by the Northern Capitalists to transport Negroes from the South and to employ them as laborers. But the action aroused the Irish laborers who felt that their standard of living was in jeopardy. In New York the Negro longshoremen were assaulted and effectively driven from work. Similar scenes were enacted in other centers such as Buffalo, Albany, Chicago and Cleveland.[24] Even during the Reconstruction Period the white skilled workers in the North refused to work in the same shops with the Negroes and the Yankee master mechanics,

---

22 Wesley, op. cit., pp. 17-20.
23 *Opportunity*, March, 1926, p. 91.
24 Wesley, op, cit., p. 99.

many of whom had been fervent abolitionists, declined to employ the colored men. In the seventies, according to Frederick Douglass, "the South offered the Negro the greatest opportunities, for all the trades were shut against them in the North."[25] As late as 1913, Dr. Haynes, writing of conditions in the North, stated: "Only in the most exceptional circumstances has the Negro been recognized as a fellow workman whose interests are common with the cause of organized labor."[26]

The World War occasioned a tremendous change. Immigration was abruptly suspended at a time when the manufacturers direly needed an abundance of laborers. In desperation, the door of the factory, the foundry, and the shop was opened to the colored. Both the Northern Negro, who had been engaged in domestic service, and the Southern Negro, driven North by the failure of the crops, entered. After the War that racial open-door policy was continued by many of the manufacturers because of the stringent restrictions placed upon immigration. Consequently, at the present time, thousands of Negroes are employed in the steel mills, in automobile plants, in foundries, and in road construction. Even a surprisingly large number are engaged as clerks in offices.[27] The City of Detroit furnishes a very concrete example of the change. In 1910, practically no Negroes were engaged in industry in that community. Fifteen years later approximately thirty thousand were gainfully employed. The Ford plants employed over ten thousand.[28]

However, that phenomenal change does not warrant the extreme sanguine hope for the Negro's future which some students have entertained. The enlargement of the Negro's opportunities was effected by exceptional economic forces. It is not representative of a change of heart. Nearly every increase in the number of colored employees in a factory has been contested. Negroes are

---

25 Wesley, op. cit., p. 212.
26 *Annals of the American Academy,* vol. 49, p. 113.
27 *Opportunity,* Feb., 1927, p. 51.
28 "The Negro in Detroit," Section III, p. 8.

seldom permitted to become overseers. Furthermore, there are many occupations which are still closed to them. The negro workman in search for employment is still handicapped by prejudice and inert custom.

Such discriminations against the colored worker, especially those which have prevailed in the North, are most serious and thwart the development of the entire colored group. If a man dwelling in the city is to live humanly, access to industry and business must be offered to him on reasonable terms. Neither is it sufficient that employment with a living wage in one restricted occupation be open. A man, to be happy, must normally enjoy the privilege of choosing, within a reasonable extent, the occupation which pleases him, the employment for which his peculiar gifts and acquired skill are adapted. He must have not only the offering of some work but the knowledge that opportunities are opened to him, the knowledge that he may labor where human needs make work for human hands, the knowledge that for his acquired skill greater remuneration will be offered, that he will be judged when superior positions are opened on the merits of his personal accomplishments. Men work contentedly at an uninteresting task if they know that their plight is due to the limited physical resources of the locality or to their own laziness or lack of skill. But if men, despite the location, despite their service, despite their skill, are forced to labor in a few restricted occupations, if the door of progress is always barred to them, then life becomes for them decidedly unbearable. Upon the closing of the door of hope follow idleness, destitution and vice. To some extent such has been the condition of the American Negro. Until recently, they have been unable to look upon a group of highly paid workmen of their own race who could furnish them a stimulating example. The aspiring colored youth has met the color line at every turn and around the masses of the race the benumbing clouds of discouragement have tended to settle and to render their labor heartless service.

Both for the present and the immediate future, the entrance of the Negro into those great reservoirs of material life in the North, such as industry and business, will depend upon the attitude of the white employer, the white employee, the trade union, and the white patron of industry. Consequently, in subsequent paragraphs, an attempt will be made to discuss the responsibility of each group.

The Employer.

One reason why the operators of large plants in the North were reluctant to employ Negroes in any capacity except that of porter was a belief that the colored man was an inefficient worker. But experiments with Negro labor during war time has dissolved to a considerable extent that assumption. The Report of the Chicago Commission stated, "Comparing the efficiency of the Negro worker and the white worker, seventy-one employers interviewed considered the Negro equally efficient and twenty-two employers considered the Negro less efficient."[29] It should be noticed that a large percentage of those Negroes were migrants from the South. During the year 1925 the National Urban League also interviewed a large number of firms employing Negro labor, such as the Buckeye Steel Casting Company of Columbus, Ohio, and the Pullman Company, which employs approximately five hundred skilled colored workers in its shops. Their reports were as favorable as those made in Chicago. The Cleveland Hardware Company said they were a "decided success." The Worthington Pump and Machine Works reported, "He has proved to be a desirable employee." The Westinghouse Electric and Manufacturing Company of East Pittsburgh found the "Negro when carefully selected and properly placed to be a dependable workman."[30] The Detroit Race Committee made a similar survey in that city and stated, "Two-thirds of the employers hiring eighty-two per cent

---

29 "The Negro in Chicago," p. 374.
30 *Opportunity,* Feb., 1926, passim.

of the men believed that their colored workmen were as efficient as white workers on the same type of work or were even more so.''[31] However, in both Chicago and Detroit the colored workmen who had migrated from the South were found to be ''slightly less regular than a like group of white workers.'' It might be interesting to note that even Gregory, the author of ''The Menace of Color,'' wrote, relative to the African Negro: ''No one, who has walked month after month with the old Zanzibar porters when they were carrying loads which with their full equipment sometimes amounting to over one hundred pounds per man, can be persuaded that a Negro cannot or will not work.''[32]

A second factor which has influenced the employer was the fear of bringing dissention into his plant. That fear has been grossly exaggerated. In many situations, if the employer seriously wished to use colored help, the friction could have been regulated without loss to the company. Numerous concerns have departments scattered throughout a city. These companies could easily, when organizing a new department, introduce colored help. The colored applicants could also be frequently introduced into established plants without serious conflict. The Chicago Commission stated, ''Information concerning relations were secured from all the 127 plants studied. Two reported race friction was a disturbing factor in their plants. Minor instances of friction have occurred but it appeared that as a rule the workers reflected the attitude of the management.''[33] In the Cleveland Hardware Company 500 of the 2994 employees are colored. The management states that they were easily assimilated and were a decided success. In that plant both the chief metallurgist and chief chemist are at the present time Negroes.[34] The Detroit Report declared, ''Employers were unanimous in stating that they had no more clashes

---

31 ''The Negro in Detroit,'' Section III, p. 13.
32 Op. cit., p. 85. Cf. ''The Negro at Work During the World War.''
33 Op. cit., p. 626.
34 *Opportunity,* Feb., 1926, p. 56.

in their plants between Negroes and whites than between groups of white workers of other national groups. One employer felt that there was less feeling between the white and colored than between certain European groups."[35]

Consequently, the question may be asked whether an employer acts wrongfully in refusing to engage Negro workmen? The Negro's need of employment is obvious and it is probable that the Negro may be engaged without detriment to the plant. So it appears that when in need of labor, whether skilled or unskilled, the employer is morally bound to make a serious effort to employ the competent Negroes who apply. The obligation arises not only from charity but from *distributive justice.*

Ethicists regard the employer as something more than a private individual. They contend that he occupies a social office, that he is the distributor of the nation's wealth. Because of his office they hold that the obligation of paying a living wage rests upon him. In just as real a sense the employer may be regarded are the distributor of the opportunities for securing a livelihood. Because of that office the obligation of giving employment to every competent applicant regardless of color rests upon him. Otherwise the Negro is denied access to the source from which a reasonable livelihood may be obtained. As Dr. Ryan observed: "In the wage contract and in every other contract that involves the distribution of the common bounty of nature or of the social product the juridical situation is vitally different from the transaction that we have just considered. The employer has obligations of justice not merely as the receiver of a valuable thing through an onerous contract but as the *distributor* of the common heritage of nature. His duty is not merely contractual but social."[36] However, if a serious effort has been made to employ colored workmen and if because of the antagonisms of the white workmen the efficient operation of the plant was proved

---

35 Op. cit.
36 "Distributive Justice," p. 371.

impossible the employer is excused from further effort. The responsibility then rests upon the employes. But the operators of industries and business which are virtual monopolies have a greater obligation to work for the introduction of colored help than those engaged in keenly competitive businesses. The employer who for no valid reason refuses to engage a Negro sins against charity and justice.

As a corollary, attention might be directed here to the superiority of the claim of the Negro over the claim of the immigrant to opportunities in American industry and business. A man's first claim to opportunities for securing a livelihood is upon the country of his birth. In the mind of the average American the immigrant's place in our industrial and commercial life has always been regarded as secondary to that of the native American. The immigrant's native country had the first responsibility. If that nation, either because of inefficient government or because of congested conditions, was unable to fulfill the obligation other countries were open to him besides the United States. Yet it has not been so generally recognized that the colored American enjoys the same right as the white American citizen. Nevertheless he was born here and is from birth an American citizen. He has the right of access upon reasonable terms to the agricultural, industrial, and commercial life of the nation. His claim is prior to that of any other immigrant regardless of racial affiliation. It does not matter whether the immigrant be English, Swedish, Irish, Polish, or German. It is a claim not only in charity but in justice.

Besides the refusal to employ Negro workmen there are other discriminations practiced by employers against the colored group. Even manufacturers who employ Negroes sometimes discriminate against them by paying them a lower wage. In the South such a practice, though not universal, is wide-spread.[37] For instance, according to a recent bulletin of the United States Department of

---

37 Weatherford, op. cit., p. 250. Woofter, op. cit., p. 112.

Labor, the average median wage for white women employed in the laundries of Tennessee is $8.30 while the average median wage given to the colored women engaged at a similar task is only $6.55.[38] In the North a few employers have adopted a similar practice. In justification of such a practice it is alleged either that the Negro's living costs are less or that he is less efficient as a workman.

A valid justification certainly cannot be deduced from the living costs of the colored group. In Philadelphia an elaborate study was recently made of the expenditures of the colored migrant for food, clothing, and housing. Their expenditures were found to be practically equivalent to those of a white family of a similar class except that the expenditure for rent was greater because of the shortage of colored housing.[39] The findings of the Detroit Commission were similar to those of the Philadelphia study.[40] The statistical statements of those reports have been vigorously and accurately paraphrased in the following observation made in a publication of the Bureau of Research of the National Urban League: "The cost of clothing is no cheaper for them and the exigencies of their rough work on the one hand and a greater social life than the corresponding class of whites on the other require that their purchases be more frequent. Rental costs are actually higher for them: they pay from 20 to 50 per cent more for the same house than a white family and in spite of the acceptance of lodgers they never are guilty of the astonishing overcrowding reached by some immigrant families. They pay more for insurance because of their death rate; they maintain more churches at a greater per capita cost than other laboring populations. Because of the narrow margin on which they live they are instalment buyers and thus pay the exorbitant interest which this method of petty commerce exacts. Even amusements are more expensive.

---

38 *Opportunity*, July, 1927, p. 191.
39 *Annals of the American Academy*, vol. 98, p. 215.
40 "The Negro in Detroit," Section III, p. 46.

Shut out from so many of the public accommodations they must create their own apart from the advantage of those indirect subsidies to the poor from the taxation of larger incomes.''[41]

In the South the standard of living for a large proportion of the Negroes is much lower than that of the whites. Yet such a standard should not serve as a justification for lower wages. Their standard falls much below that which is necessary for the preservation of health, morality, and for respectable living. As for the other Southern Negroes who have improved their conditions it should be noted, as Dr. Moton observed: ''They receive the same education, read the same magazines, visit the same stores, aspire to the same standards of living, and sometimes are obliged to provide from their own pockets recreational and educational facilities which are furnished to the whites by the government. It is too much to expect that the Negro shall in all things measure up to the standards of the white man's civilization with less than the white man's pay.''[42]

The practice of paying a lower wage to the Negro than to the white is an injustice. The white workman may be assumed to be receiving only what is due to him in strict justice. But the Negro renders the same service and has the same needs and, consequently, has a claim to equal pay. Each individual should be remunerated on the basis of his personal efficiency. An even greater wrong is committed by the employer who introduces Negroes into his plant on a lower wage scale for the purpose of reducing the wages of the white workingmen. Such an employer injures the Negro by giving him less than what is owed to him. He injures the white by attempting to reduce a standard of living to which the white worker has a strict right. He accentuates and foments race prejudice by making the races competitors. He thus retards the day of final racial adjustment and does more than does any gang of hoodlums to disturb the public peace.

---

41 *Opportunity,* July, 1927, p. 191.
42 ''Cooperation in Southern Communities,'' p. 38.

The White Workman.

"The employees of an organization," wrote the editor of Forbes Magazine, "and not the employer are very largely the dictators of who their co-workers shall be."[43] That statement, though exaggerated, is suggestive of the control enjoyed by many workmen over the entrance of Negroes into industrial plants. It also explains to some extent the absence of the colored workman from industries in the past.[44]

The white worker's objection to the Negro is due partly to a sense of superiority, partly to repugnance occasioned by racial differences, and partly to a fear of the loss of the existing standards of wages and working conditions.

In any discussion of the moral character of the white employee's objection to the Negro as a fellow workman the factor of racial superiority, though it influences many people, may be dismissed without consideration because of the grave needs of the Negro. The repugnance of the white worker, however, presents the same problem and factors discussed in the treatment of segregation. Pleasant working conditions and congenial fellow workmen are factors which deserve serious consideration. The presence of a large number of Negroes in some occupations could make work rather unpleasant for many whites. Yet there is a grave danger of exaggeration. In some industries the presence of a considerable group of Negroes would not constitute a serious hardship for any white worker because of the location of the machinery. Inconvenience felt by whites from contact with a few colored people is easily overcome. In many of the building trades Negroes have been used as laborers or helpers to the craftsmen, and no protest has been made by the whites. The houswives who employ colored domestics and the business men who employ colored porters find life tolerable. In the government offices at Washington a large number of Negroes may be found working in the

---

[43] *Opportunity,* March, 1926, p. 89.
[44] Cf. Wesley, op. cit., p. 237.

same departments with whites. The Recorder of Deeds in the same city is colored and several white officials are content to work with him. The Chicago Commission found many plants where the Negroes and whites worked in the same rooms without friction. Yet to work in the room where an overwhelming majority of the employes are colored would constitute a serious inconvenience for some whites.

Consequently, any strike or walkout initiated by white workers because the management introduces a few colored employees is unjust. According to the accepted Christian teaching, strikes generally are just only when they are necessary to relieve some grave situation, such as unjust wages or bad working conditions.[45] Such conditions are not realized in the case under discussion. Such a strike is unjust, since the rights of both the Negroes and the employer are violated. Because of the fear of disturbance in his business and because of the fear of the loss of skilled workmen the employer is prevented from doing something reasonable, something which is in a sense obligatory. Thus his liberty is unjustly interfered with. The right of the Negro which is violated is the right to be free from interference through illicit means when in the pursuit of any lawful good. The illicit means in this case is unreasonable intimidation. Consequently, the white workmen who co-operate in such a movement sin seriously. Let us suppose, however, that a considerable number of Negroes are already employed in the plant and that the introduction of others would render working conditions very unpleasant for the whites. Then the white workmen might object without acting unjustly. The difference is that in this case the employees are striving to secure reasonable working conditions and the employer is forced to do something which in many circumstances would be reasonable. Neither is any right of the Negro violated, because the pressure brought upon the management is also reasonable. These

45 Tanquerey, "Synopsis Theologiae Moralis," t. III, p. 377.

last statements may be regarded by some readers as a moral compromise or as a moral straddle. Yet they appear to be logical and fully consistent with Christian principles. Moreover, that statement, despite its niggardliness, would, if accepted by white men as a moral principle, afford the Negroes a representation in industry greater in proportion than the relation of their numbers to the total population. It could correct many of the evils which the Negro now suffers as a consequence of his disbarment. It could allay prejudice and neutralize the fear which many whites have of being forced from their occupations.

The objection to the entrance of the Negro into industry on the grounds that he accepts lower wages constitutes a different problem. If the whites were receiving a fair wage and if the Negroes as a group were consciously accepting less, then opposition to the entrance of the Negro would be entirely justifiable. It would be a reasonable attempt to safeguard legitimate standards. The probability that the Negro would accept less remuneration than a white worker in a Northern plant is most remote. Keen resentment has been manifested by the Negro against any discrimination in the wage scale, and the plants which practice such discriminations are characterized by constant turnovers. In standardized plants such practices are rare.[46] The white workman who alleges that fact as a justification for his objection to the Negro is frequently spreading a false propaganda to camouflage an unjust and uncharitable action.

Trade Unions.

The development of national labor organizations was contemporaneous with the emancipation of the Negro. During the Civil War many of the local associations of workers engaged in the more important trades organized national unions. But strangely, "there is evidence that the Negro was not welcome in those organizations."[47]

---

46 "The Negro in Detroit," Section III, p. 13.
47 Wesley, op. cit., p. 158.

In 1866 a successful effort was made to unite the various unions and the federation was designated as the "National Labor Union." At the first convention the attention of the workers was directed to the dangers which threatened white labor as a consequence of the emancipation of the blacks. The antidote recommended was co-operation, and the delegates were reminded: "There is but one dividing line; that which separates mankind into two great classes, the class that labors and the class that lives by the labor of others."[48] At a convention held four years later nine Negro labor representatives were present and a resolution was adopted that the "Union would know no North, South, East or West, neither color or sex." But despite those declarations abundant evidence is extant that the local unions which were members of the association refused frequently to admit Negroes. White members were even expelled because they worked in the same shop with Negroes. Before the end of a decade the National Labor Union was supplanted by the Knights of Labor. That society made drastic efforts to guarantee to the colored their place in the ranks of organized labor. But despite a brilliant development it also disintegrated and was succeeded by the American Federation of Labor.

From its origin the American Federation of Labor has assumed a very definite non-discriminatory policy toward the Negro. But the black man has received few benefits as a consequence of the policy. The organization is founded upon the principle of self-determination and in its constitution strict autonomy is guaranteed to the national and international unions. The declarations as regards the Negro have been to a large extent in the form of advice to the component unions. At the present time of the 110 national and international unions which are affiliated with the Federation eight bar the Negro expressly by constitutional provisions or by ritual.[49] In the remaining 102 unions the Negro is frequently ex-

---

48 Idem, p. 161.

49 Dowd, "The Negro in American Life," p. 22.

cluded by the policy of the locals. Moreover, several of the unions which are not affiliated with the American Federation of Labor, such as the Railroad Brotherhoods, exclude the Negro by constitutional provision. Hence, during the last sixty years the attitude of organized labor has undergone very little change toward the Negro. The national bodies have adopted non-discriminatory policies, but the locals have not only refused to accept the colored man into their ranks but they have even at times opposed the employment of blacks. During most of that time the local organizations have remained indifferent to the Negro's needs and have attempted to organize them only when the danger of the Negro becoming a strike breaker was acute.

The absence of colored men from a union may not always be traceable to an exclusion policy. Long apprenticeship, extensive education, and objections from employers may be contributing factors. Moreover, it must be recognized that there are a considerable number of local unions which make no discrimination and which accord the Negro applicant every courtesy and consideration shown to the whites. The Chicago Commission found that the proportion of Negro union members to the colored group was the same as the proportion of white union members to the white population. In some sections of the North the attitude of the local unions toward the Negro is still unsettled and, if influenced, the locals might be induced to assume a more sympathetic policy. But in the South and in border cities such as St. Louis the development of the union and the simultaneous growth of a middle class of whites has forced the Negro to surrender the control which he formerly possessed over the skilled trades. One recent indication of the animus of organized labor was that the bricklayer's union of Memphis, Tennessee, protested to the Board of Education against manual training in the schools for the Negro youth.[50]

---

50 *Opportunity*, Dec., 1926, p. 368.

The policy by which the unions either explicitly or implicitly exclude Negro applicants is absolutely condemnable. In the trades in which all employment is controlled by the union the action is a most serious and grievous injustice. The action of the labor union is an unreasonable use of force against the Negro. It is equivalent in many instances to standing at the door of the factory with a club. Whatever was said about the obligations and responsibilities of the employer and the employes is applicable to the trade unions. Especially the officials and others who dominate the policies sin seriously by countenancing such action.

Business and the Patron.

What was said above about the obligations of the employer and the employee in industry applies also to those persons associated with business houses. The denial of an entrance to those places injures not only the individual applicant but also the entire race. For if the colored group are to develop similar institutions of their own it is necessary that they have trained men, and practically the only places where adequate training can be secured are the existing white establishments.

However, in those establishments which deal directly with the trade the attitude of the customer is an added factor. The probable risk of losing considerable patronage would excuse the management from such an experiment in a highly competitive business. But in businesses which are virtually monopolies the employer is bound to strive to use colored help regardless of the objections of the customer. Indeed, the objection of the customer in many instances is most arbitrary and unreasonable. People permit Negroes to serve them in hotels or in dining cars; people entrust their children to the care of colored nurses; and people engage colored chauffeurs. Yet they object to making a purchase of gloves or of a coat from a colored saleswoman. The customer who objects to a clerk (or to a waiter for that matter) sins not only against charity but also against justice. The reason is the same one which has been advanced frequently throughout this essay: by such a practice the Negro's right to be free from unreasonable interference is violated. Moreover, it is probable that customers have even an obligation to support those business houses which are striving to open a place for the Negro. Dr. Ross, writing of the obligation of the consumer toward the labor conditions which prevail in a factory or store, said: "If he, the customer, can conveniently buy goods made under just conditions rather than under bad conditions and the price is no higher, then he is bound to do so."[51] Likewise, it would seem that a customer is obliged to support the stores and business houses which are employing colored help.

Prejudice has forced the colored group to organize businesses of their own. The refusal of white insurance companies to write insurance policies for Negroes has occasioned the development of strong Negro insurance companies which, during the last fiscal year, have paid approximately three million dollars in claims.[52] The same is true, though, to a lesser extent, of banks, barber shops, restaurants, tailor shops, and retail stores. Those ventures have prospered greatly despite serious handicaps such as lack of credit, lack of training in business, and at times the distrust of their own people. The recent organization of the National Negro Finance Corporation for the purpose of assisting Negroes in business indicates even a wider growth in the near future.

These racial businesses do not constitute a justification for the refusal of a place in the white commercial world to the Negro. Their fullness of development is dependent upon the Negro receiving a training elsewhere. At best they are only a partial and temporary substitute. For the great industries and businesses are woven into the warp and woof of the nation and the Negro's fullness of opportunity will be realized only when he has unrestricted entrance to them all.

---

51 Ross, "Consumers and Social Reform," p. 108.
52 Reuter, "The American Race Problem," p. 245.

In spite of the successes mentioned above, the Negroes are still allowing many splendid opportunities among their own people to escape. The officials of the Atlantic and the Pacific Tea Company in Washington have never found it necessary as means of retaining colored patronage to use colored store managers. Also, as Professor Dowd observed, "Even in the largest of their colonies the stranger seldom sees a prosperous or attractive-looking Negro store. In the midst of the colony or on the outskirts are found enterprising Italians, Jews, and Greeks who flaunt their wares before the Negro and capture a large share of his patronage."[53] By such neglect the Negro is failing to tap a great source of wealth and he is also delaying his entrance into the great businesses of the nation.

One reason for the apparent failure to develop such businesses in the past may be that too much attention and time has been spent complaining against discriminations and segregation, and not sufficient time and energy has been given to the study of the opportunities which lie about them. It was said by one of their own race: "The reason for the lack of solid achievement on the part of native New England Negroes is to be explained in terms of their attitude rather than their lack of aptitude. Circumstances have placed them in a position of perpetual dependence. They look for help from without rather than from within."[54]

---

53 Dowd, op. cit., p. 22.
54 *The Harvard Graduate's Magazine*, June, 1926, p. 10.

CHAPTER VIII

POLITICAL AND CIVIL DISCRIMINATIONS

The wrongs committed against the Negro in industry, agriculture, and business deeply affect the life of almost every colored person. However, until recently the average Negro has been more concerned about the violation of the rights which he enjoys as a citizen. An abiding conviction remains with him that if his civil and political injustices were rectified his condition would be immeasureably improved. The moment of those rights relative to the amelioration of the Negro's condition has, in the judgment of some students of the Negro problem, been greatly exaggerated. Nevertheless, since they assume such prominence in the Negro's mind, serious attention must be given to them.

I. The Negro and the Vote

History of the Disfranchisement

Prior to the Civil War a few Negroes voted in various parts of the country, but the great masses of the colored people were denied the use of the ballot not only by Southern, but even by Northern legislatures.[1] At the outbreak of the War they were allowed to vote in but four states—Maine, Massachusetts, New Hampshire, and Vermont.[2] Several years after Lee's surrender the Negroes by the enactment of the Fourteenth Amendment to the Constitution were made citizens of the United States and of the States in which they resided. Four years later, since even that constitutional addition did

1 Johnson, "The Development of State Legislation Concerning the Free Negro," p. 24.
2 Brooks, "Political Parties and Electoral Problems," p. 363.

not prevent the Southern States from restricting the ballot to the white citizens, the Fifteenth Amendment was devised and enacted. That Amendment guaranteed to the Negro the right to vote under the same conditions as the white man. After its passage the Northern States gradually undertook the task of correcting their discriminatory statutes in order to bring them into harmony with the Federal Constitution. At the present time the Negro residing in the North is as free in the exercise of the franchise as any white citizen. Without opposition or molestation he may go to the polls and cast his ballot.

In the South all the States which had seceded, except Tennessee, refused to ratify the Fourteenth Amendment, although it was proposed as the condition for their readmittance as States into the Union. Those States objected to the Amendment because citizenship was conferred upon their former slaves, because when it was adopted ten States were unrepresented in Congress, and especially because by it practically every white political leader of any prominence was disfranchised. Yet the Amendment did not, as some erroneously assume, render obligatory the immediate bestowal of the franchise upon the Negro. A choice was offered: either the franchise was to be given to the Negro or the basis of the State's representation in Congress was to be lowered.

When those States refused to approve the Amendment, Congress divided the South into five military districts and instructed the officials of the army to assemble in each State a convention for the purpose of drafting a new State constitution and for the purpose of selecting a new legislature. The delegates to the convention were to be chosen at an election in which every male citizen regardless of color or former condition of servitude would be permitted to vote. But the prospective voter was obliged to take an oath which had been designed to exclude many of the former Confederate soldiers. The conventions were, also, instructed that the new State constitutions must confer the right of franchise upon the freedmen and that the new legislatures must ratify the

Fourteenth Amendment. As a consequence of the arrangement the former slaves not only voted but they were, also, elected to important offices. In some instances they gained complete control over the governments because practically all the whites who had been trained for the task of government were disfranchised. Under the protection of Federal troops and under the guidance of dishonest politicians from the North the illiterate freedmen attempted for almost a decade to govern the Southern States. The Fourteenth and Fifteenth Amendments were ratified and a lurid carnival of misrule was enacted. Public funds were squandered on a gigantic scale and dishonesty was reflected in almost every public act. But the responsibility for the situation should be placed not upon the Negro, who was illiterate and untrained, but both upon the Northern politicians who used the Negro as a pawn to promote their personal interests and also upon the great mass of Southerners who failed to show even the slightest disposition to adopt a progressive and humane attitude toward the freedmen.[3]

Constantly throughout that period the white Southerners protested vehemently against the prevailing conditions and against the exercise of the franchise by the freedmen. While the Federal army remained they were powerless to effect a change. After a decade the North tired of constant intervention and recalled its soldiers. Immediately upon their withdrawal the native whites by the use of force and intimidation regained control of the various State governments and by the use of the same weapons prevented the entire colored population from voting during the remaining years of the century.

At the turn of the century many thoughtful Southerners began to realize that the use of force as a means of preventing the Negro from voting was generating serious evils. Such palpable flouting of the law occasioned considerable uneasiness. Also many white officials, enamoured of the practice, were attempting to use the

---

[3] Harworth, "The United States in Our Times," passim.

same weapons against inimical white factions. Under the inspiration of the more thoughtful group the State constitutions were revised and ingenious legal devices were substituted for physical violence as a means of keeping the freedmen from the polls.[4]

These devices assumed the form of tax, property, and educational tests for the prospective voter. Practically all the revised constitutions of the Southern States insisted upon the payment of poll taxes before the election. Several States demanded, also, the ownership of approximately $300 worth of property. Many required that the applicant give evidence of his ability to read and to write. Georgia and Mississippi exacted the ability to read and to interpret the State constitutions. As a consequence of these additions to the various constitutions the Negroes, being poor and illiterate, were disfranchised. But since many whites would have been disfranchised, also, another series of clauses were added to the constitutions. These clauses, which have been roughly designated as the "grandfather clauses," permitted an applicant, disfranchised by other restrictions, to vote if he had been a voter or a soldier in 1866, or if he were the lineal descendant of such a soldier or voter. The "grandfather clauses," however, have either expired or have been rendered inoperative by decisions of the United States Supreme Court. The tax and educational qualifications, though, are still enforced.

At the present time not only the illiterate, but even the educated and industrious Negro is barred from the polls by the enforcement of these provisions because their administration has been placed in the hands of local registration boards possessing wide discretionary powers. Those boards resort to many subterfuges to admit white applicants and to exclude the colored.[5]

Recently, in some localities there has been devised another scheme of exclusion, the white primary. In many of the Southern States the Democratic Party has pos-

---

4 Murphy, "The Basis of Ascendancy," p. 26.
5 Woofter, "The Basis of Racial Adjustment," p. 164.

sessed such complete ascendency that the primary at which the candidate of that party is chosen is virtually the election. In recognition of that condition several white groups have endeavored to induce the Democratic Party to restrict its membership to the white race. In several States such restriction of membership in the Party was even rendered obligatory by special acts of the legislature. Obviously, as a consequence of such a policy, the Negro qualified to vote was practically disfranchised. In justification of the practice it has been contended that the Democratic Party being a private organization could determine as it pleased the qualifications for membership. That device, though, has been partially nullified by a recent decision of the Supreme Court. A statute of the State of Texas was declared invalid which permitted only whites to vote at the Democratic primaries. "States," the Court declared, "may do a great deal of classifying that it is difficult to believe rational but there are limits and it is too clear for extended argument that color cannot be made the basis of a statutory classification affecting the right set up in this case."[6]

Prior to the announcement of that decision of the Court the white primary was regarded by many political observers as the most effective method of excluding the Negro.[7] Frank Kent, a student of national politics and a prominent publicist, has observed: "Not only has the law forbidding any but whites to vote in the primaries a strong psychological effect in keeping the Negro away from the general election but with his own parties holding no primaries and the general election of no consequence there is not the slightest inducement for him to register and he does not try. He has lost the habit of voting. He is out of politics, because there is no place where or time when he can participate without complete futility."[8] The same author has listed the causes of the

---

6 Nixon v. Hendon, Oct. Term, 1927, n. 117.

7 N. A. A. C. P. Report, 1926.

8 "The Great Game of Politics," p. 136.

Negro's failure to vote in the following order: the white primary, the poll tax, the educational qualifications, the selfishness of white Republican leaders, the strength of white public sentiment against Negro participation, and the habit of not voting.

The exact number of Southern Negroes who vote at the present time is difficult to estimate. In sections where there are two vigorous parties, such as West Virginia, Maryland, Kentucky, Tennessee, and parts of Virginia, a considerable number vote. In the city of Baltimore over 28,239 are registered. In other sections the number of Negroes who vote is very small. However, Woofter declared that approximately 3500 Negroes are registered in Atlanta, 2000 in Savannah, and 1000 in Jacksonville.[9] Kent maintains that only 595 are registered in the entire state of Louisiana.

Fundamental Moral Principles

The denunciation of the Fourteenth and Fifteenth Amendments by Southern demagogues and the denunciation of the disfranchisement of the Negroes by the Northern politicians have been favorite themes for those respective groups. Yet, before any judgment is passed upon the moral validity of the Amendments or the morality of the existing disfranchisement, several ethical truths should be recalled which are valid regardless of any constitution or law.

In the first place it should be noted that the privilege of voting is not a natural right. It is a civil or a political right which is received from the State. Such is the teaching of the Catholic theologians and the opinion of American students of politics. Professor Brooks has written, "At the present time political scientists generally regard suffrage not as a natural right but as a right conferred by law in the discretion of the State which may widen or curtail it if the highest interests of the State require."[10] Just and beneficent governments have

9 Op. cit., p. 163.
10 "Political Parties and Electoral Problems," p. 355.

flourished in the past the subjects of which were not permitted to vote. Man can occasionally attain his end and reasonably develop his personality without possessing such a privilege. That truth may be more thoroughly understood if it is recalled that the State is not a contractual society which men are free to enter but a necessary institution. When a State or government is duly established and when it is functioning for the common welfare the subjects of the territory are bound to submit to it. They are not free to withdraw assent or obedience.

However, the subjects do possess the power of designating the form of the government and of agitating for a change in form if it would actually promote their welfare. The existing governments are, also, bound to cooperate in a change if it is necessary for the welfare of all classes. In early times monarchical forms of government were prevalent. Such governments, because of the ignorance of the masses alone were able, despite the abuses, to preserve order and to prevent chaos. Gradually, however, as the people developed and as the tyranny of the rulers became more apparent, the desire of changing the form of the government to that of a democracy became prevalent. The democratic form of government, by giving the subject some control over the appointment and recall of officials, offered a check against such abuses. But the right of the franchise so characteristic of democracies came not from the subject but from the government. It was intended to assist the government to promote its end.

Democracy connotes the participation of the people in the government. A democratic government is by its very nature bound to strive to distribute the franchise so that all the competent citizens may have a voice in the selection of the officials. Yet such a government is not free to distribute the franchise to every person within its boundaries regardless of their qualifications. Rather the distribution must be made according to a principle of the moral law which is most fundamental to the activities of any State; the distribution must be for the common good, it must be made in such a manner that the public order and peace will be preserved, that the natural rights of all will be protected and that all will have equal opportunity. Consequently, Father Vermeerch in summarizing the teaching of Catholic theologians, states: "The right of suffrage is the legal and onerous power of designating rulers by whom, at least in part, a republic is governed. Hence, in its distribution concern must primarily be had for the common good and secondarily for the equal distribution of the right." [11]

The confirmation of that principle may be found in the practice of every successful democracy. Commonly the franchise is denied to those who have been proved dishonest, and to strangers. At the time our Constitution was adopted very stringent suffrage qualifications were enforced by all the States. Those patriots, whose sagacity and whose devotion to democracy modern Americans reverence, had raised the qualifications so high that less than one-half of the population was eligible to vote.[12] The tendency to give it almost universal distribution was occasioned by the struggle of the various political parties to increase their respective memberships. Today a reaction has set in and the wisdom of such a wide distribution is being challenged.

The Validity of the Constitutional Amendments

It is the practice to lament the enactment of the Fourteenth and the Fifteenth Amendments to the Constitution of the United States. Undoubtedly the time and the circumstances of their enactment were unfortunate. Other arrangements better adapted to promote the welfare of the Negroes were possible. The Northern politicians in promoting the passage of those provisions were deeply concerned about perpetuating the supremacy of their party. Yet if the Southern States had assumed

11 Vermeerch, "Questiones de Justitiae," p. 81.
12 Brooks, op. cit., p. 362.

a more conciliatory attitude the laws would have probably never been passed.

But such regretful broodings are not helpful, for the legal enactment of any other arrangement is morally impossible. Moreover, under present conditions when even the possibility of the Negro becoming a ward of the Government does not exist, and when the Federal Government is offering assistance for their agricultural and industrial training, no vital objections can be raised to those clauses of our organic law.

Persistently the Fifteenth Amendment has been criticized on the ground that it jeopardizes the common good by placing the ballot in the hands of illiterate Negroes. Actually, the franchise is not bestowed upon all the Negroes. The right of the States to impose reasonable qualifications is fully recognized. The State is only forbidden to disfranchise a citizen solely upon the basis of color. The Amendment prohibits only the disfranchisement of competent colored citizens. In objection to that statement it is often asserted that the law assumes a condition which is contrary to fact. It is objected that the Negro is mentally and morally incapable of performing the functions of a competent citizen and that consequently the ballot should not be entrusted to him. Such an opinion is contrary to the facts. In the earlier chapters sufficient evidence was adduced to show that the average Negro possesses the power of acquiring under the proper environment the mental and the moral qualifications requisite for the beneficial use of the ballot. Furthermore, the Negro was born here and since he has no memory of Africa he is free from any objectionable attachment to his original homeland. His education, his temperament, his ideals, his language, his attitude toward law are entirely American. His standards of living are to a considerable extent those of the section of the United States in which he resides. During the World War he gave sterling evidence of his devotion to

America. Not once during those days did anyone seriously challenge his Americanism.[13]

There are Southerners who, although admitting that the Negro possesses potentially the requisite moral and mental qualifications, condemn the Amendment on the ground that our government is a white man's government in which no Negro may take part. Such a contention has no foundation in our organic law. There is no evidence available that this continent was entrusted by Providence to the control of Caucasian. Such an objection is to a large extent, pure sentiment. Practically the only reasonable basis upon which it may be grounded is that the participation in the government of two groups differing so strikingly in appearance occasions friction and works to the detriment of the public peace and the common good.

The common good would possibly be better promoted if the Negroes, without objection, would permit the whites to rule and if the whites could be trusted to render full justice to both groups. Yet, such a Utopian condition does not now exist and probably never will exist upon this earth. Such a condition surpasses the powers of fallen nature. Today if the common good and the welfare of all racial groups is to be adequately promoted the Negro must have some opportunity of exercising the franchise. It is the only permanent means by which he can secure full justice and complete self-development. Interracial commissions are helpful in ameliorating gross injustices, but in the last analysis all men, being inclined toward selfishness, favor their personal and group interests. Hence, it is only when the Negro possesses some political influence, only when the qualified Negro is allowed to designate government officials that the Negro completely receives the proportionate share of public school funds and of governmental assistance. As Oldham observed: "Deprived of political influence an unfranchised class finds itself helpless

---

13 Woofter, op. cit., p. 159.

to obtain redress or to defend itself against injustice. Public men may admit the injustice. But it is not a question that any political party can afford to take up; it can win no votes while it would be certain to lose many. The monopoly of power which the white race claims for the purpose of defense cannot be prevented from becoming an instrument of aggression and oppression. Experience has proven how easily is the passage from the contention that no Negro shall vote, to the contention that no Negro shall learn and that no Negro shall labor."[14]

The Fifteenth Amendment has been condemned because it would ultimately place the control of public office in several counties of the South in the hands of the Negro and would lead to the loss of white supremacy in those sections. If the qualifications were made reasonably high and adequately enforced upon both groups, such a situation would not arise for several generations. People, when they try to peer beyond that period, are staggered with the possibilities of Negro rule because they think of the Negro as he exists in those sections today or because they think in terms of the Reconstruction Period. Such mental associations unfairly confuse the issue. If despite high qualifications the Negroes should gain control in later years it would mean that the moral and mental standards of the entire Negro group in those sections had been raised. It would mean that the Negro of that period would differ from the Negro today. Hence, it is wrong to observe with approval, as Dowd does, that if every Negro in South Carolina and Mississippi could read and understand all the constitutions in the world, the white people would not allow them to control their governments.[15] Such an attitude is largely a matter of sentiment. It is one for which no allowance can be made in a moral discussion.

The assertion that the Negro, irrespective of education, will always be incapable of governing himself or

---

14 "Christianity and the Race Problem," p. 190.

15 Dowd, "The Negro in American Life," p. 108.

others is also gratuitous. It is unfair to cite his abuse of power in the Southern States during the Reconstruction Period, or to cite conditions in Haiti, or Liberia. For the Negro when placed in control of governments in modern times has been handicapped by ignorance, lack of training, and unsettled conditions. To assert that the white race has a special aptitude for government which is lacking in the Negro is to make a statement which may conflict with the facts of modern science. Scientists have challenged the political significance of race. In popular thought nothing seems more obvious than the differences in political capacity between the Anglo-Saxon Englishman and the Celtic Irishman. Actually these differences cannot be explained on the basis of racial traits since both groups are largely one in race. Also, as Hankins observed, the America of Washington and the Federalists was scarcely the America of Jackson and the Western Democrats. Yet that difference does not imply a change in racial composition during that period.[16] Hence, the apparent differences between the poltical capacities of the Negro and the white man may be due to differences in educational opportunities and cultural histories.

Insistence upon white supremacy because the masses of the colored are illiterate and irresponsible is a reasonable proposition. Insistence upon white supremacy when the Negroes are educated and have acquired a sense of responsibility is a proposition which lacks moral justification.

The Validity of the Suffrage Qualifications

While the white citizen of the South cannot raise a sound objection to the Fourteenth and Fifteenth Amendments, the Negro cannot object to the insistence of Southern States upon high suffrage qualifications. Certainly the States are entirely within their rights in imposing tests calculated to secure an intelligent and prudent electorate. In regard to some of the Southern

---

16 Hankins, "The Racial Basis of Civilization," p. 288.

States, Senator Borah probably echoed a partial truth in declaring: "The South is in good faith seeking to work out this problem under and in accordance with the Constitution. I do not find any spirit of nullification." However, the actual formulation and administration of the qualifications are defective and need revision. To guarantee equitable enforcement they should be more stringent. The educational clauses should be corrected for the purpose of restricting the discretionary power of local boards. Yet despite their crudeness, the tests express a valid principle; namely an effort to promote the common good. Through them any correction of the existing abuses must be sought.[17]

The question may be asked: Why should the Southern States demand from the prospective voter higher qualifications than those demanded by Northern States? The answer is that they are confronted with a more difficult situation. In over 270 counties the Negroes constitute a majority and could control the government if the franchise were given without qualification. In those sections they are to a large extent illiterate, irresponsible, and untrained in self control. Moreover, since in those districts contacts with white men have been limited, and since meager educational opportunities have been furnished them, they have not sufficiently absorbed into their homes and their lives the American social heritage. Their ignorance would make them an easy prey to the demagogue.

Furthermore, stringent suffrage qualifications are necessary in the South to gain the actual co-operation of the white Southerners in any helpful and progressive policy in regard to the Negro. For the white native is strongly influenced by the vivid remembrance of an important historical event. He keenly remembers that, on one occasion in the history of the South when the Negro gained control of the State government, the public funds were squandered, and the public order and peace were gravely

---

[17] Murphy, "The Present South," p. 15.

disturbed. Some communities have not yet completely recovered from the losses which they suffered during that period. Co-operation in any policy which gives the Negro participation in political life can be secured only when abundant evidence is furnished that the participating Negro is intelligent and responsible. Insistence upon high qualifications is the only method of gaining such co-operation.

Probably the most pertinent objection which has been raised by the Negro is that, since the abuses associated with the inequitable enforcement of the qualifications are so numerous and so inseparable from the system, their welfare and the common good would be better promoted by the universal distribution of the ballot. That the Negro suffers gross and heinous wrongs because of the present inequitable enforcement is undeniable. That the Negro's welfare is an essential part of the common good, and that the white group might properly be required to sacrifice some advantages that more vital needs of the colored group might be satisfied, are propositions which are incontestable. But that the welfare of the Negro group would actually be improved by immediate universal distribution of the franchise is highly questionable. In the past, despite the numerous grave abuses, the Negro has achieved considerable progress, a progress probably greater than that which would have been secured if the blacks had been in political ascendency. Johnston, the famous English traveler, has observed, "Nowhere in the world, certainly not in Africa, has the Negro been given such a chance of mental and physical development as in the United States."[18]

Moreover, it is not certain that the abuses associated with the inequitable enforcement of the suffrage qualifications are inseparable from the qualifications themselves. As yet no serious effort has been made to correct the abuses. Such an effort is both practical and imminently probable. The growing shortage of labor

---

18 Johnston, "The Negro in the New World," p. 478.

occasioned by the recent migrations, the tendency to provide better schools, the popularity and influence of the Interracial Commission, all indicate a willingness on the part of the South to deal more equitably with the Negro. George F. Milton, the famous Southern publicist, has declared: "Many Southerners like myself favor a greater exercise of the franchise by the Negro throughout the South."[19]

As stated above, some revision of the property and educational qualifications is desirable in order to eliminate injustices and to secure a more equitable and serious enforcement. Hence a serious obligation rests upon the public officials to work for such a revision. But the present tests, despite their crudeness, guarantee an intelligent electorate and bestow upon every eligible citizen the right to vote. Consequently the practice, indulged in by local boards, of denying registration to a qualified Negro and of receiving illiterate whites constitutes a double injustice. A serious injustice is done to society because in a delicate situation the ballot is illegally bestowed upon irresponsible citizens. An injustice is done to the qualified Negro because his right to vote, secured from a presumably fair law, is violated. The injustice against the Negro assumes greater proportion when it is remembered that the ballot is the only means by which many of the wrongs against the colored race may be completely corrected.

II. Civil Rights

Besides the right to vote and the right to hold office, which are sometimes designated as political rights, there are numerous other civil rights, such as that of making contracts, and that of holding office, and in general the rights to all measures directed toward the security of either person or property. Some of the more flagrant violations of these rights relative to the Negro were discussed in the chapter on "Gross Wrongs." In racial literature, however, the term "Civil Right" is used to

---

[19] The Forum, Dec., 1927, p. 912.

designate a specific right which all ciitzens in Northern States enjoy by statute and which some regard as bestowed by common law; namely, the moral power to be free from discriminations when seeking accommodations and service in public places. It is to discriminations against that right that our attention must now be directed.

Discriminations in the North

In eighteen Northern and Western States the Negro is guaranteed by special statutes the right of entrance to any public resort and also immunity therein from all discriminations.[20] Much of that legislation was enacted in the final quarter of the last century and it was most desirable. For occasionally such discriminations left the Negroes in a condition of serious need; more frequently they exposed them to the vexing inconvenience of making a long and tedious search for resorts which would receive them. The legislation was passed to give them protection at a point where it was sorely needed.

Despite the enactment of that special legislation the Negro of this generation finds that he is confronted with almost as many restrictions as those which barred his father in public places in the North and the West. Hotels, restaurants, and theatres resort to innumerable tricks and subterfuges to exclude him; and in the courts such subtle discriminations are proven only with great difficulty and expense. Furthermore, even in instances in which flagrant discriminations have been clearly proven, white juries have refused to convict a white defendant.[21] Truly because of the growth of the Negro population in the North these discriminations do not now deprive the Negro of the essential necessities of life. Nevertheless, they continue to occasion a sense of privation and discomfort. That discomfort and chagrin deserves serious consideration in any moral discussion.

The objection may be made that feelings such as those of being dishonored or having one's self-respect flouted

---

20 Johnson, op. cit., p. 29.

21 "The Negro in Chicago," pp. 317 and 319.

are very elusive factors; that these factors are so arbitrary and so unreasonable, so indicative of a pathological state of mind, that they should receive no serious consideration. It is true that people, at times, imagine falsely that their honor and self-respect are violated by practices which are entirely reasonable and moral. A separation which implies equality and which guarantees equal accommodations cannot, if necessary, give reasonable cause for offense despite the feelings of some people. Yet a separation which implies the superiority of one group can give offense if the basis of the separation is not ability but an arbitrary physical trait, such as color. Hence the Negro has reasonable cause for taking offense from many of the discriminations practiced in the North. Moreover, his vexation has a more fundamental foundation than the violation of his honor. His chagrin is, in a large part, caused by a genuine and serious privation.

To lead a normal and reasonable life man must satisfy not only essential but also conventional needs which have been created by the accepted standards of living.[22] The cultured white man of this generation finds it necessary, if he is to be reasonably happy, to enjoy the privilege of frequenting high-class hotels, theatres, and restaurants. The same is true of the educated Negro since he receives the same education and since he is nourished on the same social life. Yet the Negro group, because of limited financial and social resources, cannot furnish its members such opportunities; the refined Negroes are forced to seek admission to the theatres, restaurants, and hotels patronized by the whites. But frequently those institutions are closed to the Negroes, or if they are admitted they are forced to accept such an inferior position that they must experience a feeling of being slighted and insulted. Such discriminations occasion veritable tragedies in the lives of many Negroes. To be forced always to seek a restaurant on the rear street, to be placed always at a table in some alcove, to be compelled

---

22 Ryan, "The Living Wage," p. 127.

always to accept a seat in the gallery of a theatre, to be denied access to every respectable and standard hotel, to be driven constantly to tax one's ingenuity to secure a reservation in a Pullman, are conditions which would occasion in every man, and the Negro is no exception, anger and despair. A white person probably can never fully realize the anxiety and hesitancy which the Negro experiences almost daily in trying to satisfy conventional needs.[23]

The immediate cause of the practice of excluding the Negro from public places with its grave consequences is the action of the white proprietor. But, obviously, the more ultimate cause is the objection of white people to having contact with Negroes under such circumstances. So the question may be asked: Is there any justification for their objection?

The White Patron

If the majority of the patrons of a restaurant or a theatre were Negroes attendance at that resort would probably constitute a serious inconvenience for the average Northern white. Yet it is clearly no serious inconvenience for white persons to eat in a restaurant where several colored people are dining. Exception is seldom taken to colored persons when they are employed as waiters or as chefs. Equally irrational is the objection to the presence of colored guests at a hotel since objection is not made to colored maids and porters. Theatres, however, present some difficulty because of the closeness and the length of the contact. In Chicago the proprietors of several theatres testified that patrons complained frequently when they were seated next to Negroes.[24] Yet among the more refined classes the objectionable factors which are usually associated with the laboring classes are absent. Possibly in a few exceptional instances a white person might suffer some inconvenience. But the mere

---

23 Cf. Oldham, "Christianity and the Race Problem," p. 167.

24 Op. cit., p. 318.

presence of a Negro in an orchestra seat should not occasion discomfort.

The statement is rather commonly made by whites that although the presence of a few Negroes in a theatre or restaurant does not constitute a serious inconvenience their opposition to even a few Negroes is, nevertheless, reasonable. For if a few Negroes were admitted their friends in turn would begin to patronize the establishment and would crowd the place until they comprised a majority. A condition would eventually be created which would cause the white patrons considerable inconvenience.

Actually there is no likelihood of a majority of Negroes attending most resorts patronized by the Northern whites. In the North they constitute a small proportion of the population, and they are congested into a restricted residential area. The majority of the group being poor and uneducated would drift toward the restaurants and "movies" in the Negro section. Only the educated and cultured class would attempt to patronize the resorts frequented by the white people. Moreover, in any group of colored people many economic classes are represented. The Negroes, who would attempt to patronize white resorts, would go to those attended by the corresponding economic class of whites. So the number of Negroes who would be thrown in with any white group would be small. People mistakenly think that the admission of one Negro would constitute an opening through which a black deluge would pour.

Consequently, the white person who in a hotel, restaurant, or theatre objects by word or action to the presence of a Negro *sins seriously* against charity. For charity normally binds a person to refrain from any action which could reasonably offend a neighbor or which could make his life uncomfortable. That such an action by a white person would reasonably offend a Negro is certain. That such an action constitutes a serious offense is evidenced in the effects. There is applicable in this matter a principle which has been used extensively in problems of justice; namely, the gravity of an injury should be deduced not only from the quantity of the damage done to the wronged individual but also from the damage which must accrue to society if such an action is not gravely prohibited.[25] Likewise, the seriousness of the sin against the Negro should be determined not only by the quantity of the chagrin or the inconvenience experienced by a single Negro but also by the unhappiness and the bitterness which the entire Negro group must experience if such an action is not gravely forbidden.

What may be said of the actions of those persons who discontinue attendance at a public resort simply because a few Negroes are present? Normally a man may change his patronage without violating any commandment. A considerable freedom in the choice of merchants is necessary for reasonable living. But in the case in question such an act would seem to constitute a violation of the precept of charity. For a man is usually bound to refrain from any action which discomforts his neighbor if he can do so without great inconvenience. In this instance, the slight inconvenience experienced by a white man because of his contact with a few Negroes appears insignificant as compared with the humiliation, chagrin, and privation which the Negro must experience if the white man is permitted to withdraw. For when white people withdraw the proprietor is forced from economic necessity to exclude the Negro.

The White Proprietor

Since the proprietor of a public resort is held responsible by the civil law in the North for the exclusion of the Negro, and since he controls to some extent the admission of the patron and the actions of the patron, it seems that the proprietor is morally bound to make a serious effort to admit Negroes to his establishment. In those resorts which are free from competition, such as standard high-class hotels or theatres, there is scarcely any reason which would justify the proprietor for adopt-

25 Tanquerey, "Synopsis Theologiae Moralis," t. III, p. 285.

ing a policy of exclusion. To refuse a Negro admission under such circumstances is both unjust and uncharitable. The Negro has received from the State the right to enter into any public place and that right, though a civil one, is as sacred and inviolable as a natural right. In competitive businesses a serious effort, also, should be made by the proprietor to admit the Negro. For a loss of patronage will not always follow because of the presence of a few Negroes. Proprietors are, at times, too prone to exaggerate the sensitiveness of white patrons. At the 1927 convention of the National Conference of Social Work held in Des Moines, Iowa, the fifty colored delegates were given accommodations in the leading hotels of that city. It is not recorded that any of the hotels in question suffered a loss of patronage.[26]

However, if it is certain that a considerable loss of patronage will follow from the presence of Negroes, then the owner or proprietor may refuse to receive Negroes. For the Negro would gain nothing by the admission, and the proprietor would be forced out of business since the Negro group would be too small to support him. To insist upon the recognition of the Negro's right under such circumstances would be unreasonable. It is an instance in which the axiom is exemplified; "domino irrationalibiter invito non fit injuria." All rights are limited by reason. Moreover, the method used by the proprietor must be consonant with the respect to which the Negroes are entitled. Breaking dishes which the colored patron has used and spoiling his food are obviously added injustices and are not permissible. Attendants and waiters frequently sin against charity and justice by the many discourteous actions which they manifest toward the colored race.

The remedies for such discriminations must be found ultimately in the education of the white people through the press, the school, and especially the Church, to the realization of the unfairness, the uncharitableness, and

---

26 *Opportunity*, June, 1927, p. 185.

the injustice involved in their actions. Court actions in the past have been almost prohibitive because of the cost and the trouble involved. But lately in some localities, the powerful Negro organizations have financed the litigation for exceptional cases and by gaining favorable court decisions have given many of the proprietors evidence of the practicability of the law. Possibly such a method may be the means of correcting many of the discriminations. The Negroes, however, should use prudence in entering such resorts especially if identical resorts are operated for the colored people. An antagonism might be aroused which would make contacts difficult in more important fields such as industry and business.

People at times regard the attempt of the colored group to enter high class hotels and theatres as mere impertinence, as forwardness, as boldness. They forget that the Negro is struggling for the recognition of a great need. They forget that the Negro believes that he is carrying on a crusade not only for himself but for the generations to come. They forget that often it would be much easier and more agreeable to surrender to existing conditions. Not a desire to be associated with whites but a sense of self-respect and duty forces many of them to carry on the unpleasant struggle.[27]

Discriminations in the South

In many of the Southern States a situation exists which alters considerably the morality of such contacts. It is probable that the Negro does not legally possess in those sections any civil right of entering a place of public resort. In Tennessee and Delaware the proprietors of public resorts enjoy explicitly from the State constitutions the same privilege of excluding persons as that enjoyed by the owners of private dwellings. In the other Southern States the courts would probably hold that the existing custom or practice of separating the races had abrogated the right which the American citizen receives

---

27 Du Bois, "Darkwater," p. 224.

from the common law. Nor is the Negro guaranteed any legal protection or immunity by the Fourteenth Amendment. For the Federal courts have recognized as valid the segregation of the Negroes in trains and schools.

Also, it is very questionable whether in those sections any natural right of the Negro is violated. The separation of the races is accepted by both groups as an established custom. The Negro, if equal facilities are offered, does not feel as keenly that his honor and self-respect are compromised. Furthermore, the actual privation or hardship experienced by the colored group is less. The colored group is proportionately greater there than in the North and the resorts for the colored are more numerous. And the proprietor, if he serves the colored group, exposes himself to a greater danger of losing his patronage. So the principles and conclusions presented above in the discussion of segregation would appear to have application in these instances. Yet in this matter as in segregation the separations should be reduced to a minimum and then enforced so that they do not imply the superiority of one race over the other.

There are some discriminations in the South which are unjustifiable. For example, it seems to be clearly wrong to refuse the Negro admission to concerts, or high class entertainments, or to insist upon even the refined group going to the gallery. For those needs of the refined colored class cannot be satisfied within the Negro group and it is humiliating to be forced into the gallery or to any other position which connotes inferiority. In this age when blacks and whites are meeting as equals in interracial conferences some practical adjustment honorable to the colored group could probably be made. In many of the border cities the colored group is relatively small and yet the discriminations are as drastic as those in a Southern city. Under such circumstances the discriminations are entirely condemnable. In Washington, for example, the whites are entirely content to sit beside the blacks in the Congressional Library but they refuse to sit beside them in the theatre.

CHAPTER IX

CORRELATIVE OBLIGATIONS

The successful remedy for many of the serious evils afflicting the American Negro group will come, some students believe, from a great moral crusade which will sweep through the nation appealing to the ideals of men, a crusade which will phrase its message not in terms of duty but rather of voluntary service, a crusade which as a national revival will appeal to man's nobler emotions. Very probably the existing movements for improving racial relationships and for correcting gross injustices would be given a definite impetus by some such crusade. Yet, while some of the flagrant injustices may be uprooted, it is very unlikely that an immediate and permanent reform of existing conditions will be thus effected. Such crusades are necessarily short-lived because of their emotional intensity. The existing evils will be corrected only after years of tedious effort since they are twined about the established customs of the people and in the mental habits of individuals. Possibly the working of economic and social forces such as the migrations of the colored group may improve considerably the Negro's condition.

Any permanent reform, in as far as it is influenced by the deliberate actions of Christians, will come only as each individual and each social organization acquires a fuller knowledge of his or its definite and detailed obligations toward the Negro in the daily contacts of life. The conduct of an individual through a long period of years is motivated and controlled not by vague ideals or generous impulses but by a clear concept of particular obligations and by a genuine desire to fulfill them. The emotions of men are fickle, and ideals frequently evaporate when an attempt is made to condense them into particular actions. For the numerous and prosaic actions whose repeated performance gives substance to life, duty and a sense of obligation are the main springs of action for the average individual. The majority of men make a serious, consistent effort to fulfill only those actions which they recognize as personal duties. It is appropriate, then, that in this final chapter of an essay on the moral implications of the color line attention should again be directed to the obligations of individuals and of social organizations.

The duties of several social organizations and of individuals acting in a social capacity have been delineated in the preceding chapters: the duties of the Federal and State governments, the duties of the Southern railroad officials, the duties of real estate boards, the duties of employers and trade unions. Various obligations of white individuals in contacts such as those in schools, in hotels, and in factories have also been examined. Unfortunately space does not permit the detailed restatement which those various obligations deserve. Other responsibilities have yet to be examined: the obligations of the press, of the Church, and especially those of white individuals toward the capital sins of the race problem.

The Capital Sins of the Race Problem

Since the time of Gregory the Great there has been placed in every formal treatise on Christian morals a special section which treats explicitly of the seven capital sins. But the subject-matter of that section is not the examination of seven formal sins but rather of seven tendencies to sin or seven vices which flourish in every human heart. Those vices are thus designated and an entire section is given to a discussion of them because they are the sources of many moral weaknesses, because the individual who surrenders to them inevitably involves himself in grave and depraved moral habits which damage irreparably both the individual and the social group with which he has contact. The individual is solemnly warned that he is morally bound to suppress the first tangible stirrings of those tendencies in his heart. Unless their first flames are quickly stamped out they may blaze forth into uncontrollable passions.

Just as those great vices have ever been the sources of much personal and social immorality in like manner two tendencies flourish in many Americans which analogously may be designated as the capital sins of the race problem. They are the sources from which have flown many of the modern evils which afflict the Negro.

One capital sin is the thoughtless acceptance and repetition of unverified and disparaging rumors about the Negro. Seldom in the history of mankind has any group been more widely misrepresented, misunderstood, and handicapped by popular rumors than the American colored group. The basis of much of the prejudice which blocks the progress of the Negro is the constantly repeated assertions that Negroes are lazy, sexually loose, unintelligent. Actually all Negroes are not lazy, sexually loose, or ignorant. Sufficient evidence was presented in earlier chapters to indicate that Negroes when placed in a helpful industrial system work as energetically as white men. From numerous sources may be gathered testimony that many Negroes live chastely despite social forces which have drastically thwarted the development of Christian home life among them. The ever increasing number of American Negroes who are making valuable contributions to literature and science disproves the assertion that they are necessarily unintelligent. To state that all colored men are bent upon attacking white women is arrant nonsense.

The practice indulged in by white individuals of carelessly repeating those statements is morally wrong, for the human mind was created for the reception of truth, and the organs of speech for its conveyance. The chronic acceptance and dogmatic repetition of fallacious statements about an entire racial group is an abuse of the natural faculties, a deordination of nature. Furthermore, it is uncharitable and unjust. The individual who on insufficient reasons judges that another person is immoral makes a rash judgment and according to the teaching of the theologians commits an injustice.[1] Likewise each colored individual has a claim upon white persons that they suspend judgment until moral weakness has been definitely detected in the individual. The white person who, on the strength of a general assumption, concludes that every Negro is immoral sins by rash judgment. Furthermore, the theologians declare that the person who asserts that all the members of a community live dissolute lives injures by calumny the innocent members.[2] Similarly, the white person who carelessly states that colored persons are lazy or dishonest commits an actual injustice against many Negroes, for talented and competent Negroes are tremendously handicapped by such assertions.

Because such statements are carelessly and thoughtlessly uttered they seldom in themselves constitute a serious moral offense. Nevertheless, each white person is under a serious obligation to strive to correct such an evil tendency just as he is under an obligation to correct any other bad habit, since the colored group suffers drastically as a consequence of such a practice. For evidence a white individual in the North need not look beyond his personal experience. Many Northerners can testify that their original desire to assume a helpful, charitable, and liberal attitude toward the colored group was decidedly altered by the disparaging observations made by persons who purported to know. Those persons who in careless conversations are accustomed to advocate force in the solution of race problems should meditate upon the observation of the Chicago Race Commission that, "The moral responsibility for race rioting does not rest upon hoodlums alone but also upon all citizens, black and white, who sanction force or violence in interracial relations, or who do not condemn and combat the spirit of racial hatred thus expressed."[3]

---

1 Tanquerey, "Synopsis Theologiae Moralis," t. III, p. 158.
2 Noldin, "Summa Theologiae Moralis," t. II, p. 663.
3 "The Negro in Chicago," p. 644.

The second capital sin of the race problem is the aversion or antipathy felt by the average white individual toward the Negro. This aversion, as stated in the third chapter, is not instinctive. It is rather the result of several tendencies common to all men, intensified by easily distinguishable physical traits and heightened by habitual association. Though the existence of the aversion cannot be questioned neither may one challenge the capacity of a white individual to suppress the repugnance, at least, in regard to a small number of Negroes. Because of convention or necessity many people employ Negroes as maids, as cooks, as chauffeurs, and overcome any sense of repulsion which they formerly entertained. Evidence even exists that the unpleasantness experienced from close contact with many Negroes can be controlled by individuals working under powerful motives. Missionaries, physicians, and merchants live happily though placed amidst a large colored group.

That feeling of aversion experienced by white people has occasioned almost every Negro many hours of bitterness and unhappiness. It has been a passion which has begotten acts of injustice and uncharitableness. That aversion has in part prompted white men to object to the presence of the Negro in trains, in schools, in hotels, and restaurants; that aversion has prompted white men to object to the Negro as a fellow workman in a factory or in an office; that aversion has influenced white men so strongly that Reuter has declared that the race problem, "is primarily a matter of difference of physical appearance;"[4] that aversion may be compared to these capital sins, these passions, such as pride, jealousy, and lust which lurk in the human heart and which have often spread misery throughout a community.

Although that aversion is not voluntary, and although it frequently thrives without any deliberate action on the part of the subject, each white individual is under obligation to attempt to suppress it. Man is not re-

---

[4] Reuter, "The Mulatto," p. 18.

sponsible for the feelings of jealousy, envy, and hatred which spring up in his heart. Yet, if a man is to live happily, if he is to avoid serious acts of uncharity and injustice, then he must strive to suppress those impulses and evil feelings. As Noldin observes, "If they are not repressed they can easily be approved by the will and so degenerate into acts of hatred."[5] Likewise, if a white individual is to avoid committing actual sins against the Negro, if the great social evils which now handicap the colored group are to be abolished, then an earnest attempt must be made to suppress feelings of aversion and antipathy. The attempt to control them will involve tedious efforts and sacrifices, it will tax the patience and endurance of many stout hearts. Yet such a struggle should not discourage the genuine Christian. "For the kingdom of heaven suffereth violence."

The Press

The power and the control of the press over American public opinion challenges comprehension. Few men have the opportunity or the leisure to investigate and to study public questions. Their knowledge and information is drawn entirely from the columns and sometimes the headlines of the newspapers. Furthermore, not only their knowledge but even their opinions, their convictions, their attitudes have origin in the press. Only the exceptional man has the courage to think and to reason over his attitudes. Some being deliberately conscious of their deficiency seek an authority, an instructor. The newspaper is ever ready to act the role. But the great majority being incorrigibly imitative are concerned about entertaining convictions and attitudes identical with those of their countrymen. They mold their opinions after those expressed in the newspaper which intrudes itself daily into their homes. They surrender themselves to the newspaper not because of its dogmatism but because people accept it as an accurate mirror

---

5 Summa Theologiae Moralis," t. II. n. 700.

of public opinion. Few social forces in the United States possess a power over the opinions of the citizens equal to that of the press.

In regard to the Negro Race in the United States the newspapers in the past used their power and their influence to the detriment of that group. They have exploited the crimes and weaknesses of the erring members of the colored group and have been for the most part silent in the matter of the Negro's cultural achievements. It is a tendency of the human mind to generalize, to attribute to a group the vices and weaknesses which a few members manifest in their actions. In the case of the colored group that tendency is accelerated by the easily discernible physical traits. The newspapers have fostered and nourished that tendency of the white man. They have featured the crimes of the colored and emphasized in heavy type the racial affiliation of the culprit.

In this connection the Chicago Race Commission examined 1338 Negro news items which appeared in the leading newspapers of that city throughout a period of two years. It was found that less than 75 of that number dealt with constructive subjects, while the others featured the criminal actions of Negroes.[6] Similar disproportionate conditions could undoubtedly be discovered in other large cities. The inevitable consequence of such a policy of the press is that the prejudice and the antagonisms of the white group are accentuated and that at times the public peace is seriously jeopardized. Causal connections between the policy of newspapers and race riots have definitely been proven in the instances of the riots in Atlanta, East St. Louis, Omaha, and Washington.[7]

The publishers and the editors of those newspapers which persist in featuring the crimes of the Negro sin seriously against charity and justice. For as a direct consequence of their action prejudice is accentuated and the public peace is jeopardized. It has been objected

---

6 "The Negro in Chicago," p. 540.
7 Woofter, "The Basis of Racial Adjustment," p. 243.

that theirs is the liberty to publish the racial affiliation of any criminal just as they publish the facts about other crimes in which the public is interested. Yet such an objection is misleading. Their liberty to publish information about crimes is not unrestricted. Its only justification is that the public welfare justifies or warrants such action. The public welfare is the rule by which the liberty of the press is bound and limited.[8] Obviously, in the presence of such critical relations as those which exist between the colored and white races in the United States, the public welfare is not promoted by printing news which may occasion a riot and which will undoubtedly increase the burden of the innocent Negroes and handicap their progress. More effective and saner methods of protecting the nation from the Negro criminal element exist. The police records are reliable barometers which can warn the public officials if additional measures need be taken. The extent to which some of the sensational papers have flagrantly violated the rights of the colored group creates a genuine moral question whether one may be permitted to sell or to purchase such papers.

Of late years, however, a decided change among the more responsible dailies has been noticeable. Many of them are endeavoring to give greater space to the achievements of the Negro in the arts and sciences, and over five hundred publications have agreed to receive the constructive information released by the Interracial Commission. There is, also, evidence of a determined policy on the part of the conservative papers to minimize the racial factors in their stories of crimes. Robert E. Eleazer in a statement of the conditions of race relations for 1926 declared that some newspapers are rapidly becoming most powerful influences for better relations.[9]

---

8 Noldin, op. cit., vol. II, n. 651.

9 *Opportunity*, Jan., 1927, p. 16.

The Church

Christ imposed upon the first rulers in His divinely-established Church and upon their successors to the end of time a solemn obligation: "Going therefore teach ye all nations, baptizing them in the name of the Father and of the Son and of the Holy Ghost. Teaching them to observe all things whatsoever I have commanded you."[10] That obligation involved the raising of the image of the Cross in the market places of strange races, the constant heralding of the glad tidings of the Gospel to the poor and the oppressed of every land, the ministration of the sacraments, the fountains of Divine Life, to all men irrespective of color or race. That obligation involved also the arduous task, which some people overlook, of applying the moral teaching of Christ to the complicated practices and social customs which new civilizations and modern inventions have introduced into the lives of men.[11]

Ministrations to the Colored

To the primary task of bringing to the American Negroes the light of the Gospel and the ennobling power of the sacraments the Church has generally been faithful. In the French and Spanish colonies founded during the sixteenth century the clergy were constantly concerned that the Negroes should not only be baptized but also trained in the Christian mode of living.[12] One historical event which strikingly suggests that the declarations of the Spanish and the French clergy were not mere platitudes is that the first native American to be clothed in the purple of a Catholic bishop was a Negro. Francisco de Luna Victoria, the son of a Negro slave, was consecrated Bishop of Panama in 1751. High moral and intellectual qualifications have been required in every age by the Church of the man to whom she entrusted the crosier. That a Negro of that period

---

10 Matthew, XXVIII, v. 19, 20.
11 Cf. Ryan, "Declining Liberty," p. 181.
12 Cf. Johnston, "The Negro in the New World," p. 90, also *The Student World*, July, 1926, p. 30.

could possess such qualifications reflects the existence of an elaborate system of religious training.[13]

In 1828, in the City of Baltimore a special school was opened by a Catholic priest for the purpose of educating the colored children.[14] The establishment of that school deserves emphasis because it was probably the first of the sort in the United States and because the attempt of the abolitionists to erect a similar institution in New England, a few years later, met with a storm of protest. The people of Maryland, however, had been prepared for such an action since they had been accustomed to the spectacle of the scholarly and pious Sulpician Fathers devoting their entire energy to ministering to the spiritual needs of the black slaves. It is even more astonishing that, while the education of the Negroes was proscribed in many Southern States, the teachers in that school were refined colored women, refugees from San Domingo who had been educated in Paris.[15] In 1831, in order that the missionary work among the colored might be more effectively conducted a group of educated colored women were organized into a sisterhood, the Oblates of Providence, and upon them were bestowed the same ecclesiastical honors which the Church showers upon white women who pledge themselves to virginity. In the few other sections of the South where the Catholic missionaries, despite prejudice, gained entrance, earnest efforts were also made to minister to the Negro. In Charleston, for example, Bishop England opened a school for the blacks.[16]

There is evidence, however, that about 1840 the Catholics, or at least many of them, succumbed completely to the existing beliefs and attitudes prevalent in the South. They continued to welcome the blacks to their churches and to urge the reception of the sacraments, but they grew cold and indifferent to the ideals and the leadership which had glorified their earlier history. Little

---

13 *Records of The American Historical Society*, vol. 35, p. 107.
14 *Records of the American Catholic Historical Society*, vol. 35, p. 120.
15 *Woodson, "The Education of the Negro,"* p. 98.
16 Idem, p. 183.

concern was shown for the education of the slave or for the improvement of the physical surroundings and the social conditions which drastically influenced his moral life.[17]

After the close of the Civil War the Catholic missionary work among them acquired a new impetus. The bishops at the Second and the Third Plenary Councils passionately pleaded with their flocks that they give generously of their funds and their service for the religious instruction of the freedmen. At the present time besides three hundred colored sisters there are several entire sisterhoods of white women that are devoting all their activities to working among the American Negroes—the Sisters of The Blessed Sacrament, the Franciscan Sisters, the Holy Ghost Sisters. Other orders such as the Sisters of Mercy, and the Sisters of Divine Providence are represented in the work by individuals. There are, furthermore, several congregations of priests which are devoting their lives entirely to preaching and to ministering to the colored—the Josephite Fathers, the Holy Ghost Fathers, the Fathers of the Society for African Missions. Other religious orders such as the Society of the Divine Word, the Jesuits, and the Marists have priests delegated to work among the colored.[18]

Until recently the majority of the members of the Catholic Church in the United States have dwelt in the North and have been of the poorer classes. Their meager financial resources were for a long time overtaxed in the work of erecting suitable edifices. Because of that former financial impotency they have never acquired the practice of looking beyond the immediate horizon and concerning themselves with the needs of distant people. As a consequence, the men and women who have consecrated themselves to the labor of bringing to the oppressed American Negro the consoling light of the Gospel and the sanctifying power of the sacraments

17 *Records of the American Catholic Historical Society*, vol. 35, pp. 325-344.

18 Report of the Catholic Board for Mission Work among the Colored People, New York, 1925.

have been forced to endure privations and physical hardships which equal and in some instances surpass those suffered by missionaries in China and India. What is needed, then, is a greater number of laymen and laywomen who will give more freely of their wealth and services to the support of Catholic missions. In that respect Catholics have failed. Father La Farge, an associate editor of America, has written: "Looking at our past record we notice a contrast that cannot but make us uncomfortable. With all fair credit to their more abundant share of leisure, opportunity, and the world's wealth, Protestant laymen have certainly given their time, means and personal service to the welfare of the colored race to an extent unheard of among American Catholics."[19]

The members of non-Catholic sects have always comprised an overwhelming majority of the white Christians of the nation. Theirs, then, was the greater opportunity of Christianizing the Negroes. The thoroughness with which that opportunity was grasped depended greatly upon the locality. When the various colonial assemblies declared that baptism did not carry with it freedom from the bonds of human slavery, serious efforts were made by the various religious leaders to baptize and to receive the Negro slaves into their churches. The Negroes were especially welcomed at the annual camp meetings and revival services conducted by the Baptists and Methodists. But in the South after 1830, Woodson states: "Other forms of religious instruction were denied them and, with the exception of a few, those despised people were generally neglected and left to die as heathen. In 1840, there were in the South only five colored Sabbath Schools with an attendence of about 1400."[20]

The weaknesses and failings of the Southern Christians were more than compensated by the devotion and zeal of their Northern co-religionists. Prior to the Civil War they agitated strenuously for the abolition of

---

19 *America*, Nov. 16, 1926, p. 110.
20 Woodson, "The Education of the Negro," p. 180.

slavery. Later hundreds of young men and women from splendid New England homes followed the Federal troops southward and nobly dedicated themselves to the task of giving the freedmen religious training and education. Moreover, even those who remained at home made sacrifices for the cause. The work of those young missionaries was subsidized by generous donations from Northern congregations. Many of the institutions for the higher education of the Negro which exist in the South owe their origin to the labors of those crusaders from the North and the support of Northern funds: such, for example, are Hampton Institute, Atlanta University, Fish University, and Shaw.[21]

The Condemnation of Racial Wrongs

The obligation of the Christian Church toward the Negro is not completely fulfilled by the attempt to bring to the blacks the message of the Gospel and the sacraments of Christ. Since many of the evils which afflict the Negro group in the United States are the consequence of the unjust and the uncharitable actions of Christians, the Church has an obligation to emphasize the moral character of those actions.

The true Christian Church has never felt free to confine her preaching to the enunciation of general moral principles. Rather the peculiar vices and the particular crimes which have tended to flourish in various generations have always been explicitly, particularly, and concretely condemned. Not only murder and dishonesty but particular species of those crimes were denounced. Not only gluttony and impurity, but specific tendencies of those vices were castigated. In the heyday of drunkenness a very definite campaign against that vice was inaugurated by the Church. When the practice of divorce began to grow common the Church inaugurated a definite propaganda against the evil. In the latter part of the nineteenth century when the evils of the industrial revolution became strikingly evident, Pope Leo XIII

21 Reuter, "The American Race Problem," pp. 265, 311-317.

wrote the famous encyclical letter, "On the Condition of Labor." In that monumental document the Pope declared that he was morally bound, because of his office, to describe in the lives of various classes the new duties which the industrial revolution had occasioned: the duties of the capitalist, the employer, the craftsman, the trade union.

All those evils are not due to the actions of Christians. Yet many of them exist because well-intentioned Christians have failed to recognize their obligations toward the Negro.[22] Many of them exist because Christians have not received detailed instructions in interracial matters. Many of them exist because religious teachers in the United States, departing from the tradition and practice of the Church, have preached only general principles, because the teachers have assumed, what the true Church has never assumed with her intimate knowledge of human nature, that the individual members would apply the general principles to concrete proplems. Consequently there is incumbent upon the religious teachers and upon the representatives of the Church in America a grave and urgent obligation to indicate the wrongfulness of many of the deeds perpetrated against the Negro.

Despite those failures of the past every fair-minded person must recognize that at present many serious efforts are being made by the various denominations not only to promote racial good-will by organizing interracial conferences, but also to define in detail the application of Christian principles to the Negro problem. That tendency is manifested both in the South and in the North. Speer has written: "No one can read the literature on this subject of twenty years ago and then the literature which the South is producing today without realizing the immense progress that has been made in the courage and justice and hopefulness with which the Christian people of both races are meeting this real

22 Cf. Hammond, "In Black and White." p. 209,

crisis."[23] Possibly the most thorough work along those lines has been done in Sunday-schools and religion classes. In that field the work has acquired such moment that it has occasioned the publication of a large number of religious text books which treat specifically of racial contacts.

The Methodists, for example, have a text for young people entitled, "The Negro in American Life." Robert E. Speer, a prominent lay reader in the Presbyterian Church, has produced a work, "Race and Race Relations." The Missionary Education Movement of the United States commissioned Basil Matthews to write, "The Clash of Color." For work in Y. M. C. A. assemblies, "The Negro from Africa to America," was written by Weatherford, the president of the Southern College of the Y. M. C. A. The National Board of the Y. W. C. A. sponsored an "Outline for Discussion Courses on Race Relationships in the United States." All those texts are weak because of their vagueness. Yet they have value because they constitute an attempt to correlate Christian obligations and the Negro problem. They point out the method the Christian Church must adopt if she is to fulfill her obligation.

In accordance with the policy of the Church in other matters specific injustices and wrongs against the Negro should occasionally during the year be denounced from the pulpit. It would be helpful if on one Sunday during the year a sermon was given which treated exclusively of the Negro as the subject of rights and as an object of Christian charity. In the parochial schools and Sunday-schools one week might be specially devoted to the study of interracial problems. In the text books used for religious and moral instruction the duties of the white person toward the Negro should be more explicitly treated. The religious press should also strive to spread information about the progress and the achievements of the colored group since such data is a powerful solvent of

---

23 Speer, "Race and Race Relations," p. 348

prejudice. Co-operation could be urged with the National Urban League, the Interracial Commission, and other organizations which are genuinely working for the improvement of the Negro's condition. As Pope Leo XIII wrote, "While firm in the affirmation of dogma and refusing all compromise with error it is Christian prudence not to repulse but rather to be able to enlist the help of all honest men in the pursuit of good whether individual or above all social."[24]

Segregation in Churches and Parochial Schools

Finally, the Church and its ministers must preach not only by word but also by action. It is proper that in every section where large groups of Negroes dwell that separate parishes should be established for them. Many of the colored, just as the French, the Germans, and the Polish, prefer to worship by themselves. When racial groups in a nation differ strikingly the Church has always permitted them to form separate congregations. Thus it is possible to minister more efficiently to their spiritual needs.

It is wrong to deny to the Negro, who finds it more convenient to attend a white church, a place in the building or to insist upon his going to the gallery or remaining in the rear pew, or taking any other place which necessarily connotes inferiority. Such a practice gives offense to a neighbor in the very citadel of Divine Love and is contrary to the spirit of brotherhood which, according to the Scriptures, must be evidenced in the Churches. "Despise ye the Church of God and put them to shame that have not?" asked St. Paul of the Corinthians.[25] St. James wrote: "My brethren, have not the faith of our Lord Jesus Christ of glory with respect of persons. For if there shall come into your assembly a man having a golden ring, in fine apparel, and there shall come in also a poor man in mean attire, and you have respect to him that is clothed with the fine apparel, and

---

24 Cf. Moon, "Labor Problems in France," p. 171.
25 I Corinthians, XI, v. 22.

shall say to him, 'Sit thou here well;' but say to the poor man, 'Stand thou there or sit here under my footstool': Do you not judge within yourselves, and are become judges of unjust thoughts?"[26]

The official head of the Catholic Church, the Pope, has had so far no occasion of commenting upon the practice of segregating races in some American Churches. Yet in view of his recent severe condemnation of the discriminations practiced between the native and missionary clergy in Africa there can be no doubt about his attitude. Father Moslein, the distinguished Passionist missionary, who has labored among the colored people of Texas for many years, has written: "What would be the style of a letter of guidance if the Pope would write to the bishops of the United States in regard to the Negro members of the Church may be readily inferred. Taking into account what he wrote for the guidance of bishops, whose field of labor is in the midst of social conditions far below those of colored people in the United States, it is more than likely that his instructions would be that the color line must be abolished at the earliest possible date wherever it works a grievance for Catholics of color in their standing in the Church, and that they must be accorded every right and privilege enjoyed by their white brethren in the Faith."[27]

The same statement, to a considerable extent, is applicable to church schools. Special parochial schools for colored may properly be established in connection with a colored parish to meet a definite educational need. In Southern States in which the attendance of blacks and whites at the same school is prohibited by law or by strong public opinion that is entirely beyond the control of the Church, the separation of the children into racial groups is inevitable. Yet in the Northern or in the border States the compulsory separation of the races by ecclesiastical authorities, or the refusal of a place in a Catholic college to a colored applicant seems to be an

---

26 James, II, v. 1-9.
27 *The Sign*, October, 1927, p. 136.

act of disloyalty to Christ. The children are thus trained by the Church to make racial distinctions, when social organizations are assuming a leadership in the opposite direction. Moreover the colored children are thus frequently wronged by being denied a Christian education, an education which the Church values so highly that she refuses at times the sacraments to the parents who fail to send their children to Christian schools.

Furthermore, the act of discriminating against the Negro in churches, while sinful in itself, has added malice because of the grave effects of such a policy. These consequences are so serious that they clearly outweigh other factors, such as discomfort, for which allowance was made in the discussion of the morality of segregation in trains and other public places.

By segregating the races within church buildings the authorities, instead of fulfilling their solemn obligation of discouraging discriminations, actually prove recreant to their office. Their preaching will be not only barren but harmful as long as clergymen insist upon closing the doors of the churches to the Negro or insist upon reserving for them the rear pews. Congregations are influenced more by what they see than what they hear. One can scarcely hope for improvement in racial relations during the next generation when children even in the sanctuary of life are acquainted and trained in discriminations. If any form of segregation is unjust, if any discrimination is uncharitable, if any judgment made in the preceding chapters enjoy validity, then the practice of compelling Negroes to accept inferior positions in Christian Churches constitutes a serious wrong. One very practical effect of the exclusion of the Negro from the Church is evidenced in the retort made by Samuel Gompers that the trade unions could not be condemned for racial discriminations when they were practiced by the churches.

The hindrance of conversions is another evil consequence to such discriminations, especially in the Northern and border cities. The Negroes, because of the poverty and the burdens which they bear, offer a most fertile field for the sowing of the spiritual seed. But the practice of segregation in churches not only hinders the efforts of the missionary but even causes many a colored Catholic to waiver in his faith and allegiance.[28] Such practices furnish arguments to the cynical white publicists and educators who ridicule Christianity before the colored youth. Moreover, not only colored persons but even white people are alienated from the Church by such practices. They insist upon judging the sincerity of the Church by her attitude upon racial matters, especially in this generation when humanitarian and non-Christian social groups are laboring so zealously to bring the races together. "From all appearance of evil," St Paul wrote, "refrain yourselves."

The objection is proposed that to worship in the same church with Negroes constitutes a very serious inconvenience for many whites.[29] It must be admitted that some whites experience discomfort when forced to worship with blacks in a small church. But the discomfort has been grossly exaggerated and can be controlled at least for one hour on Sundays. The evidence for that statement may be found in the large number of white people who insist upon attending Mass on Sundays in colored churches either because of the music or because of the convenience to themselves. Even if the discomfort were greater the Christian would be bound to submit to it while in church because of the consequences. Unfortunately, in the past, the self-control of the Christian seems to have been completely eclipsed by that of unbelieving merchants, physicians, and social workers.

The Obligations of the Negro

Throughout this essay emphasis has been placed upon the rights of the Negro. But in the agitation for those prerogatives there is danger that the duties of the col-

---

28 Cf. O'Brien, "The White Harvest," pp. 95-113.
29 "The Negro Pew," Boston, 1837.

ored people may be forgotten. Many of the false generalizations about the Negro have a foundation in unpleasant traits which were fostered by slavery and which persist in some proportion in the colored people today.

Indolence, petty dishonesty, untruthfulness, vulgarities, and indifference toward domestic relations characterize an uncomfortably large number of Negroes. Those traits when present in a white man occasion a prejudice against him on the part of other whites. Sobriety, industriousness, and honesty wins from even the most prejudiced American respect and tolerance. The colored people, out of charity to themselves, have an obligation to strive to eradicate those weaknesses.

A considerable group of the colored people have not developed sufficiently the virtue of cleanliness. Poverty is frequently accompanied by uncleanliness as a handmaid, but they are not inseparable. Without the expenditure of large sums of money much could be done to improve the appearance of the dwellings of Negroes. In Washington, for example, there are streets in the colored section which are well paved and on which the houses were in reasonably good condition a few years before their occupancy by the colored. Since they have been rented by the colored, rubbish is often strewn about the front yards, crude signs adorn the door posts, and the window shades are frequently torn. They have permitted a pleasant district, which the Germans or the Scotch would have kept immaculate, to deteriorate. The Detroit Racial Committee declared: "A general campaign of education is necessary to urge on colored people the special desirability of keeping their houses painted and their yards in attractive condition so that colored sections should compare favorably with sections occupied by white persons of corresponding economic status. A similar emphasis upon the personal appearance and demeanor of colored people and their children is equally desirable." [30]

---

[30] Publications of Detroit Bureau of Research, March 10, 1927, p. 4, n. 108.

Upon the shoulders of those Negroes who are accepted as leaders has fallen a mantle of office which carries with it solemn obligations. Upon those men will depend to a large extent whether the Negro's character is to grow in strength; whether the colored group are to acquire those simple, chaste, and industrious habits of life upon which all influential civilizations have been founded. Upon them, also, the decline of prejudice will be partially dependent. Their policies, their programs, their labors, though not as picturesque as those of a general on the battlefield or that of the diplomat in the council chamber, will affect the masses more vitally; and if successful their glory will be greater because their battle against such intricate social evils requires greater skill. But in direct proportion to the gravity of their office and the breadth of their opportunity is the gravity of their obligation to study carefully the effects of their policies upon the genuine welfare of their people. Frequently, if sincerely concerned about the permanent happiness of their race, they will be forced to persist stoutly in the advocacy of unpopular measures.

One moral virtue which is almost indispensable to the leader is prudence; the prudence which, forgetful of personal popularity and a doctrinaire philosophy, actually concerns itself with the welfare of the masses; the prudence which seeks the means best calculated to improve the well-being of the people with the least possible damage.

Completely satisfactory conditions are not won by one blow. They are gained only after many struggles and compromises. Since the whites are more powerful than the Negroes both in numbers and influence the enactment of any measure of improvement will depend in large measure upon the good-will of the former. At the present time many influential whites of the South, while insisting upon the separation of the races, would cooperate in any movement for the improvement of colored schools or residential sections.[31] Consequently, any racial leader who would attempt to carry on the struggle against segregation to the extent that the co-operation of such people might be lost would do his race considerable harm and deprive them of services which affect their life much more vitally than does separation in schools or trains. Prudence is built upon compromises, and compromises are not necessarily disgraceful or wrong.

---

31 Cf. Mims, "The Advancing South," p. 277.

WORKS OF REFERENCE

The subjoined list includes the books and the articles which were used more frequently by the author in the preparation of this volume. The editions noted are those to which he has had access and which are cited in the text.

Alphonsus, St. de Ligorio,
Theologia Moralis, Augustae, 1891.

Allport, Floyd,
Social Psychology, New York, 1924.

Aquinas, St. Thomas,
Summa Theologia, Rome, 1894.

Bailey, Thomas,
Race Orthodoxy in the South, New York, 1914.

Ballerini-Palmieri,
Opus Theologicum Morale, Prati, 1899.

Basil, Joseph,
The Clash of Color, New York, 1924.

Bennett, Frank,
Forty Years in Brazil, London, 1914.

Blyden, Edward,
Christianity, Islam, and the Negro Race, London, 1887.

Boas, Franz,
The Mind of Primitive Man, New York, 1922.

Bogardus, Emory,
Fundamentals of Social Psychology, New York, 1924.

Bouquillon, Thomas,
Theologia Moralis Fundamentalis, Bruges, 1890.
De Virtutibus Theologicis, Bruges, 1890.

Brackett, Jeffrey,
Notes on the Progress of the Colored People of Maryland, Baltimore, 1890.

Brawley, Benjamin,
A Social History of the American Negro, New York, 1921.

Brooks, Robert,
Political Parties and Electoral Problems, New York, 1923.

Brownson, Henry,
The Works of Orestes Brownson, Detroit, 1885

Bryce, James,
South American Observations and Impressions, New York, 1902

Bucceroni, Ianuarius,
Institutiones Theologiae Moralis, Rome, 1915

Burgess, John,
Reconstruction and the Constitution, New York, 1902.

Busch, John,
"Race Attitudes of Children," *Religious Education,* January, 1926.

Cappello, Felix,
Tractatus Canonico-Moralis de Sacramentis, Augustae, 1923.

Cathrein, Victore,
Philosophia Moralis, Friburg, 1895.

Carlyle, R. W. and A. J.,
A History of Medieval Political Theory, London, 1923.

Carpenter, Niles,
"Nationality, Color and Economic Opportunity in the City of Buffalo," *U. of Buffalo Studies,* June, 1927.

Carriere, Jos.,
De Justitia et Jure, Louvain, 1847.

Channing, Edward,
A History of the United States, New York, 1925.

Chicago Commission on Race Relations,
The Negro in Chicago, Chicago, 1922.

Cochin, Augustin,
The Results of Slavery, Boston, 1863.

Childs, B. S.,
The Negro of Lynchburg, Virginia, Charlottesville, 1923.

Commission on Interracial Cooperation,
Cooperation in Southern Communities, Atlanta, 1921.

Corrothers, James,
In Spite of the Handicap, New York, 1916.

Cox, Earnest,
White America, Richmond, 1923.

Cronin, Michael,
The Science of Ethics, New York, 1909.

Dawson, Warrington,
Le Negre aux Etats-Unis, Paris, 1912.

Detroit Bureau of Governmental Research,
The Negro in Detroit, Detroit, 1926.

Dowd, Jerome,
The Negro in American Life, New York, 1926.

Dublin, Louis,
"Life, Death, and the Negro," *American Mercury*, September, 1927.

Du Bois, W. E. B.,
Darkwater, New York, 1920.
The Gift of the Black Folk, Boston, 1924.

Duncan, Hannibal,
The Changing Race Relationships in the Border and Northern States, Philadelphia, 1922.

Dunn, L. E.,
"A Biological View of Race Mixture," *Publications of the American Sociological Society*, Volume 19.

Elwang, William,
The Negroes of Columbia, Missouri, Columbia, 1904.

Estabrooks, G. H.,
"A Proposed Technique for the Investigation of Racial Differences in Intelligence," *American Naturalist*, January, 1928.

Fallon, Valere,
Eugenics, New York, 1923.

Faris, Ellsworth,
"The Superiority of Race," *Institute of Pacific Relations*, Hawaii, July, 1927.

Finot, Jean,
Le Prejudice des Races, Paris, 1921.

Garrison, W. and F.,
William L. Garrison, New York, 1889.

Garth, Thomas,
"A Review of Racial Psychology," *Psychological Bulletin*, June, 1925.

Gasparri, Petro,
Tractatus Canonicus de Matrimonio, Paris, 1904.

Gault, Robert,
Social Psychology, New York, 1923.

Gerrard, Thomas,
The Church and Eugenics, St. Louis, 1921.

Goldenwiser, Alexander,
Early Civilization, New York, 1922.

Gregory, J. W.,
The Menace of Colour, London, 1925.

Hammond, Lily,
In Black and White, New York, 1914.

Hart, Albert,
Slavery and Abolition, New York, 1914.

Helper, Hinton,
The Impending Crisis, New York, 1857.

Hankins, Frank,
The Racial Basis of Civilization, New York, 1926.

Haworth, Paul,
The United States in Our Times, New York, 1925.

Haynes, George,
The Trend of Races, New York, 1922.

Herskovits, Melville,
"Preliminary Considerations of the Culture Areas of Africa," *American Anthropologist,* January, 1924.
"Does the Negro Know His Father," *Opportunity,* October, 1926.

Inquiry, The,
And Who Is My Neighbor, New York, 1924.

Johnson, Franklin,
The Development of State Legislation Concerning the Free Negro, New York, 1918.

Johnston, Harry,
The Negro in the New World, London, 1910.

Junod, Henri,
"L'Attitude des Peuples Latins vis-a-vis des Races de Couleur," *Student World,* July, 1926.

Kelleher, J.,
"The Ethical Aspects of Boycotting," *Irish Theological Quarterly,* Volume II, 1907.

Knapp, Isaac,
The Negro Pew, Boston, 1837.

Knerick, Francis,
Theologia Moralis, Mechlin, 1866.

Kent, Frank,
The Great Game of Politics, New York, 1924.

Kerlin, Robert,
The Voice of the Negro, New York, 1920.

King, Willis J.,
The Negro in American Life, New York, 1925.

Lehmkuhl, Augustinus,
Theologia Moralis, Friburg, 1888.

Lessius Leonardus,
De Justitia et Jure, Lyons, 1612.

Le Roy, Alexander,
The Religion of the Primitives, New York, 1922.

Linton, R.,
"An Anthropological View of Race Mixture," *Publications of the American Sociological Society,* Volume 19.

Locke, Alain,
The New Negro, New York, 1925.

Lowie, R. H.,
"Psychology, Anthropology, and Race," *American Anthropologist* Volume 25.

Lugo, Joannis de,
Disputationes Scholasticae, Paris, 1868.

Marvin, F. S.,
Western Races and the World, Oxford, 1922.

McDougall, William,
Outline of Psychology, New York, 1923.

Mecklin, J. M.,
Democracy and Race Friction, New York, 1914.

Miller, Herbert,
Races, Nations, and Classes, Philadelphia, 1924.

Miller, Kelly,
Race Adjustment, New York, 1908.
"The Causes of Segregation," *Current History,* March, 1927.

Milton, George,
"Black Ballots in the South," *The Forum,* December, 1927.

Mims, Edwin,
The Advancing South, New York, 1926.

Molina, Lodovicus,
De Justitia et Jure, Moguntiae, 1669.

Mossell, Sadie,
"The Standard of Living Among One Hundred Negro Migrant Families in Philadelphia," *The Annals of the American Academy of Political and Social Sciences,* Volume 98.

Moton, Robert,
Finding a Way Out, New York, 1920.

Murphy, Edgar,
Problems of the Present South, New York, 1908.
The Basis of Ascendency, New York, 1909.

Murphy, Miriam,
"Catholic Missionary Work Among the Colored People of the United States," *Records of the American Catholic Historical Society,* June, 1924.

Muntz, Earle,
Race Contact, New York, 1927.

National Association for the Advancement of Colored People,
Annual Reports for 1926 and 1927. New York.

National Urban League,
Opportunity, A Journal of Negro Life, Volumes 4 and 5, New York.

Noldin, H.
Summa Theologiae Moralis, Oenipente, 1924.

Oldham, Joseph,
Christianity and the Race Problem, New York, 1924.

Olivier, Sydney,
White Capital and Colored Labour, London, 1906.

Olmstead, Frederick,
A Journey in the Seaboard Slave States (reprint), New York, 1904.

Page, Thomas,
The Negro, the Southerner's Problem, New York, 1904.

Petrovits, Joseph,
The New Church Law on Matrimony, Philadelphia, 1921.

Phillips, U. B.,
American Negro Slavery, New York, 1918.

Pintner, Rudolf,
Intelligence Testing, New York, 1923.

Prummer, Dominicus,
Manuale Theologiae Moralis, Friburg, 1923.

Quillin, Frank,
The Color Line in Ohio, Ann Arbor, 1913.

Reed, Ruth,
The Negro Women of Gainesville, Georgia, Athens, Ga., 1922.
Negro Illegitimacy in New York City, New York, 1926.

Reuter, Edward,
The Mulatto in the United States, Boston, 1918.
The American Race Problem, New York, 1927.

Ross, John E.,
Consumers and Social Reform, New York, 1912.

Ryan, John,
Distributive Justice, New York, 1916.
Declining Liberty, New York, 1927.

Sanchez, Thomas,
De Sancto Matrimonii Sacramento, Antwerpiae, 1626.

Schlesinger, Arthur,
Political and Social History of the United States (1829-1925), New York, 1927.

Shannon, A. H.,
The Racial Integrity of the American Negro, Nashville, 1925.

Smith, Robert,
Christianity and the Race Problem, New York, 1922.

Speer, Robert,
Race and Race Relations, New York, 1924.

Stoddard, Lothrop,
The Rising Tide of Color, New York, 1921.

Stroud, George,
A Sketch of Laws Relating to Slavery, Philadelphia, 1856.

Suarez, Fransicus,
Opera Omnia, Paris, 1856.

Tannenbaum, Frank,
Darker Phases of the South, New York, 1924.

Tanquerey, Ad.,
Synopsis Theologiae Moralis et Pastoralis, Paris, 1919.

Taparelli,
Le Droit Naturel, Paris, 1852.

Toke, Leslie,
The Housing Problem, St. Louis, 1912.

Theobald, Stephen,
"Catholic Missionary Work Among the Colored People," *Records of the American Catholic Historical Society,* December, 1924.

Tobey, James,
"The Death Rate Among American Negroes," *Current History,* November, 1926.

Thomas, W. J.,
"Race Psychology," *American Journal of Sociology,* Volume 17.

Vermeersch, A.,
Questiones de Justitia, Bruges, 1901.

Watson, Goodwin,
The Measurement of Fair-mindedness, New York, 1925.

Waffelaert, G. J.,
De Virtutibus Cardinalibus, Bruges, 1889.

Weale, Putnam,
The Conflict of Colour, New York, 1910.

Weatherford, W. D.,
The Negro from Africa to America, New York, 1924.

Wernz, Fransicus,
Jus Decretalium, Rome, 1904.

Wesley, Charles,
Negro Labor in the United States, New York, 1927.

Westermarck, Edward,
The History of Human Marriage, New York, 1922.

Willoughby, W. C.,
Race Problems in New Africa, New York, 1923.

Woofter, Thomas,
The Basis of Racial Adjustment, New York, 1925.

Woodson, Carter,
The Education of the Negro Prior to 1861, New York, 1915.
A History of the Negro Church, Washington, 1921.
The Mind of the Negro as Reflected in Letters Written During 1800-1861, Washington, 1926.

Work, Monroe,
Negro Year Book, 1925-26, Tuskegee, 1925.

Young, E. F.,
"What is Race Prejudice," *Journal of Applied Sociology,* Volume 10.